MW01714340

I dedicate the book to my juvenescent self when I was in prison learning life the hard way, discovering the power of written words.

I dedicate the book to my current self two decades later when my understanding of why man turns evil is a tiny bit better.

Who am I ?

CONTENTS

Introduction vii

THE DARK SIDE: EVIL AND ITS PERMUTATIONS.

1. What Is the Dark Side of Humanity? 3
2. The Concept of Evil. 14
3. Good vs. Bad: Is Humanity Doomed Since Its Inception? 36
4. Nature vs. Nurture: What Makes Us Evil? 54
5. The Fundamental Aspects of Being Evil: How Do You know? 74
6. The Temptation of Evil. 87
7. Morality and Evil. 100
8. Evil Actions: Who Will Take Responsibility? 118

THE PATH TO THE DARKSIDE: PUSH AND PULL FACTORS.

1. Xenophobia: Us vs. Them Mentality. 135
2. Expectations and Evil. 145
3. Tunnel-Vision: Dark Thoughts. 157
4. Temptation and Weak Will. 168
5. Social Disparity: Effect on Psyche. 181
6. Ignorance: Feigned or Real. 196

7. Hurt and Anger: The Road to Revenge and Retribution. 208

PATH TO REDEMPTION.

1. Severity of Actions: Shades of Forgiveness. 223
2. Don'ts: Victim Syndrome and Martyr Complex. 236
3. Guilt and Regret: How They Help. 247
4. Anger Management: On a Micro Scale. 258
5. Cultivation of Peace and Calm. 265
About the Author 271

References 273

INTRODUCTION

What do we as human beings wish for most when we're wronged? Oftentimes, it is justice we yearn for most. When we feel slighted, we lash out. We try to hurt the one who made us feel this way in a selfish bid for understanding. Sometimes our actions go beyond justice and edge into revenge. Hatred becomes a constant companion as we chase our assailant. We make gut-wrenching decisions, all in the name of having others understand what our pain feels like. But in making these attempts, we are lured—step-by-step—to the dark side of our psyche.

Human beings are physical beings that are connected by bonds to each other, to society, to a purpose, and to an end, as a whole. We live, we breathe, we laugh, we smile, and one day we die. We depend on each other for understanding, compassion, love, and much more. We are social creatures. A treasure is lost when a human being passes away—hoards of bonds, promises, and memories are shattered.

But… What makes a human being *a human being*? What is *being* human like?

To be human is to make our own decisions and to bear their consequences. Sometimes these consequences are good, sometimes they are bad. Some actions taken in the heat of the moment reveal things about us that we would rather hide. Other times they reveal the best of us. Sometimes, the worst people can move mountains to save others, while at other times, the best people can put their life at risk to destroy others. What prompts these actions? Is there a mysterious power that affects our actions? Does the potential for good and evil reside within us? Are we predestined to be good or evil? What power in the world prompts us to take these actions?

All of these are good questions. In this book, we will explore the effects of our inclinations, our desires, and our thoughts on our actions. We will investigate topics like cognitive dissonance, tunnel vision, prejudice, xenophobia, self-deception, and social disparity and their effects on our actions. We will discuss the vast array of feelings and thoughts that lead us to commit heinous actions. We will discuss the problem our species has with violence. We will discuss the world in which mass rapes seem like a military strategy, where the potential for creating thousands of wastelands with a flick of a finger is regarded as power, where mass bombing constitutes religious fighting, and where safety is an outlandish concept.

We will explore the biology of violence and the dark side and why we are so attracted to it. We will consider cases of human social behavior and, many times, cases of abnormal human social behavior to understand the lure of the dark side. We will try to understand the role played by aggression and competition in making us walk on a path that may not be right. We will try to understand if we can find a way back home once we've trodden this path.

Can we come back from the dark side? Is it possible to walk away when we have climbed the ladder to the other side? Is it?

There is no way to answer this question without taking all the facts into account. Cynical commentators would say that it may not be possible, that there is a point of no return, that some actions cannot be justified no matter what. They would say that we are judged not by our intention but by the way our actions affect others. They might be right. They might be wrong.

Other commentators may raise the issue of granting forgiveness to those who have committed the worst of evils not because they deserve it, but because the potential for great evil exists in all of us, and if, by any chance, we fell into this quagmire, we would have hope that someday, someone might forgive us. They could also be right. Or, they could also be wrong.

There is no single answer to these questions because the experience of each individual is very different. Therefore, in this book, we will take a great number of angles into account before we come to a conclusion. We will go through the neurobiological, psychological, and cultural aspects that lure an individual to the dark side. We will consider real-life examples and fictional stories in the course of this book to gain valuable insights into the darkest fringes of the human mind.

THE DARK SIDE: EVIL AND ITS PERMUTATIONS.

WHAT IS EVIL? WHAT MAKES US EVIL? ARE WE EVIL BY NATURE OR NURTURE?

In this section, we will talk about the dark side of humanity, what it is and what it prompts us to do. We will discuss the concept of evil and why it is disputed. We will search what makes humans evil: their nature or their nurture, by going through theories presented by various philosophers throughout the centuries such as Plato, Hobbes, Kant, and Kekes, among others. We will explore the actions of famous evil men such as Maximillian Robespierre, Pol Pot, Hitler, and Adolf Eichmann, among others, to find out the motivations behind evil actions. We will discuss the nature of evil and why it is tempting, and will conclude this section by discussing who carries the responsibility for evil actions.

1

WHAT IS THE DARK SIDE OF HUMANITY?

WHAT IF A PERSON NEVER FACED CONSEQUENCES for their actions? What wouldn't they do then? Would anything they ever do be called evil?

> "Because sometimes you have to do something bad to do something good."
>
> —Oscar Wilde.

AROUND A THOUSAND YEARS AGO, in 1162, a boy was born along the banks of the Onon and Kharlen Rivers in what is now known as northern Mongolia. This boy was born with a blood clot clenched in his fist, a sign that he would one day become a great leader. A sign that, perhaps, this boy would shed blood by the bucketful. He was named Temujin meaning, "of iron" or "blacksmith". Who would have known that in forty-five years, he would become the "Great Khan" and would murder millions of people in his quest for land, glory, and wealth?

THE STORY GOES something like this: Genghis Khan—the emperor of the Mongol empire—sought to have the Khwarazmian Empire as a trading partner on the Silk Road. He sent a 500-man caravan to the city of Otrar, but the governor of Otrar attacked the caravan and stripped it of its riches. When asked by the Mongols to make amends and return the loot, the governor refused.

GENGHIS KHAN SENT a group of emissaries to the Shah, asking for reparations to be made. In this group were two Mongols and a Muslim. Not to be outdone by his governor, the Shah had the Mongols shaved and sent the Muslim emissary's head back to the Great Khan as a gift. Little did the Shah know that he had doomed his people to a horrifying death.

Enraged, Genghis Khan gathered over 100,000 soldiers and marched onto the Khwarazmian Empire.

They captured the city of Otrar and poured liquid silver into the eyes and ears of the governor who wronged them. They enslaved the city and killed hundreds of men, women, and children. As they marched further inland, the Mongols burned entire cities, enslaved the populations of dozens of towns, and built pyramids with their severed heads to show their enemies that those who crossed them would die a gruesome death.

City after city fell under the rage of the Great Khan. His army looted and killed with wild abandon. Atrocities after atrocities piled up. At last, they came to the city of Urgench—a wealthy trading city in the Khwarazmian Empire. Fighting raged for days as the city defenders sacrificed themselves to hold their enemy back. For every step taken into the city, the Mongols lost dozens of men. Block by block, men fell. Bodies piled up like kindling ready for a fire. Mountains of dead could be seen everywhere. ... Comparing the rage of the Mongolian soldiers who watched their brethren die to a bonfire is like calling the ocean a stream.

They *hungered* to kill those who had killed their own.

FINALLY, the city fell. But... the warriors were not satisfied. They were enraged at the dishonor that had befallen them. Only more blood would satisfy their thirst. An eye for an eye. A life for a life. When the Mongols sacked the city, they took the women and children as slaves, killed every soldier that fought against them, and massacred the whole city. Hundreds of thousands of people died in that sacking, making the sacking of Urgench one of the bloodiest massacres in human history.

AFTER THE MASSACRE, the army celebrated and then moved on. They had won a great battle. They had scourged their enemy's stronghold. They were joyous.

. . .

The most surprising thing about Genghis Khan was that despite being a ruthless and cunning leader, who massacred entire cities in order to evoke terror in the hearts of his enemies, he was tolerant of all religions, supported the rights of women—it is said a woman could walk the Silk Road alone in his time and not be harmed—and was open-minded—a man who invited others to question him and present him with their arguments.

This raises the question: How could such an enlightened man not see what he was doing? He was a tyrant not because he had to be, but because he wanted to be. Many times he said to the people he enslaved that he was their punishment from God. He used this excuse to justify his actions many, many times in front of a great many people. The slightest provocation could send him into a rage that was only fed by the blood of millions.

The takeaway from this story is that even the most enlightened of people can have a dark side that prompts them to take actions that can horrify anyone. It seems everyone has a dark side, whether it is the soldiers in the army committing atrocities for their Khan, or the Khan himself enslaving and massacring people to exact his revenge.

THE DARK SIDE of humanity is the part of the inner self that lies hidden deep in the shadowy recesses of our personalities—the self that we either knowingly or unknowingly hide from even our most loved ones. The self that holds our darkest desires. In most people, this inner self is hidden, while in others, it is the driver of their actions. The dark side is not about being evil or immoral; it is not characterized by sinful acts. It just *is*. It is part of human existence—what we go through in our lives. It prompts humanity to commit actions that can be horrifying and despicable.

THE DARK SIDE steps out when we feel jealous at seeing someone happy and try to destroy them. The dark side is also there when we murder someone in cold blood without any reason or when we break down someone psychologically to further our goals.

. . .

THERE ARE many facets to humanity; some are dark, some are light, some are gray. Light is a symbol of goodness, peace, tranquility, and calm, whereas darkness is a deep void where the extremes of anger, ambition, hatred, jealousy, and envy lie in wait for prey. The gray is the area where most of humanity lurks. We bury our extremes into pits so deep within us that they become hard to find. Sometimes, these extremes peak through when we're under stress, angry, or emotional. At other times, this side of our humanity pokes out during our happiest moments.

WE HUMANS ARE COMPLEX CREATURES, driven by our ambitions, our goals, and our zeal to become better or to get better things. Countless civilizations have been obliterated from the annals of history by a dictator who thought he knew best. Millions of innocent people have perished in vengeful battles provoked by arrogant rulers. Similarly, millions have been slaughtered like sheep by armies that found them in their way. What prompted them to commit these actions? Did they not have a conscience?

It is said that absolute power corrupts absolutely. This may be true because the actions committed by leaders like Hitler, Stalin, and Genghis Khan, who had no one to question them, were astounding and unbelievable. Hitler massacred 6 million Jews in his bid for Aryan supremacy. Anyone who ever disagreed with Stalin was killed, maimed, or murdered.

And Genghis Khan killed anyone who betrayed him. He razed their cities, their homes, and their countries until not one of their people were left.

The people of the Great Khan lauded his actions as great and mighty. He was exalted and superior in his prowess. His actions were never thought of as evil or immoral. In their eyes, the betrayers got what they deserved. But what about the people who were murdered? The women who were taken as slaves? The innocent children who had become the victims in a game between two colossi? What about them? What did they think? Did they think his actions were evil? Did they curse him in their sleep, in their thoughts, and in their privacy?

Maybe they did. Maybe they did not. We will never know.

IN HIS CHILDHOOD, after his father's murder , Genghis Khan's tribe threw him, his siblings, and his mother out of the clan. The young Genghis Khan had to hunt and forage to survive; it is rumored that he had to kill his brother to get food. In later years, he was captured as a slave by a rival tribe and spent a long time there before he could escape. When he was sixteen, his wife was kidnapped and taken as wife by her kidnappers.

IT IS SAID that the Great Khan felt his heart torn out when his betrothed was taken from him. He rescued her with a team of his men and took the child she carried in her belly as his son.

. . .

All of these events must have had an effect on the Great Khan. What should have prompted empathy in him, only made him harder. Instead of being merciful, he would kill a man in a breath if he saw fit. Instead of being tolerant of other empires, he subjugated them. He never hesitated to bring his sword down on any who resisted him.

This brings us to our last lesson. The appearance of the dark side also depends on the way we live. The more we are exposed to the darker elements of life, the more we will favor the dark side. This means that an individual who has been psychologically damaged in some way, especially during childhood, is more likely to succumb to the dark side than a person who has had none of these experiences.

2

THE CONCEPT OF EVIL.

"The mind is its own place, and in itself can make a heaven of hell, a hell of heaven..."

—John Milton, Paradise Lost.

ALAN FRIEDMAN WAS A SOON-TO-BE-FATHER, A drunkard, and on his best days, a husband. Alan worked as a floor layer with several construction companies throughout the city he lived in. He worked for days on end, tirelessly, going from one job to another as if the hounds of hell were set loose on him. He was friendly with everyone. Sure, he had a bit of a drinking problem, but who did not? He was a good floor layer, one of the best.

Alan's hair looked like a sparrow's nest, his beard struck out in odd directions as if he had been electrocuted, and he looked like a man deep in the throes of liver failure. Nevertheless, he could rattle off complex mathematical calculations within a moment of hearing them. Construction crews regarded him as a novelty, and structural engineers tested him at every turn. But deep down, Alan had always wished to be an M.D.

He dreamed of fixing people, of helping them, and of telling them everything was going to be okay. He dreamed as he lay the wooden floor. When he was done working, he would go home to his wife and smile and laugh with her, and for a while, his world was bright. He would touch her stomach, feel the kick of the child he had created, and sigh in wonder, imagining what this child would be like.

. . .

He wanted to be the best father possible. Not like his own. But he was terrified. Terrified that something would go wrong.

He had just sat for a while, a bottle of water in his hand when a crew member asked for help in hauling concrete blocks.

The thing about Alan was that he was kind. He went and helped . But the other member put the block down too fast. Alan's fingers were crushed. He stared at his hand numbly. The realization had not reached him yet. He tugged his hand out with the help of his crew members and went to get it fixed. He realized as the doctor stitched his hand together that he would not be able to lay floors for a while. He did not know where he would get the money to support his child.

Alan returned home for solace, but his sweet wife was not there. He needed consolation. He needed peace desperately. There was only one option left. He stole a bottle of whiskey and took a shot. Peace. Finally. He drunk some more, and before he knew it, his surroundings were hazy. His head spun. He heard someone come into the house. He heard someone call his name.

Everything was blurry.

But one scene was emblazoned in his mind: his wife gasping, lying on the foot of the staircase in a spreading pool of blood as he stood on top of her, a broken bottle in hand. He watched the blood pour around the glass shards in her neck. She seemed to be gasping his name, her eyes wide with fear and sorrow. Horror overtook him as he realized what he had done.

Is Alan evil?

By all means, he seemed to be a good person. He helped people, he loved his wife, and he had friends who admired his work. Is he evil because he was drunk? Is he evil because he killed his wife while he was drunk?

. . .

In the eyes of the law, Alan committed manslaughter. He killed his wife. He was lucid enough afterward to realize what he had done. He tried to make it better, but he couldn't. Does his drunken behavior make him evil? He recognized that he had done wrong. Does this recognition make him an evil person or does it make him a wrongdoer?

Let's say Alan had a psychological problem. Maybe he had bipolar disorder or depression. What then? How will he be characterized? Again, is he a wrongdoer or is he an evil person?

Let's take the case of another person named Todd. Todd lived in an area very far away from any main town or city. His closest neighbor was ten miles away. One day he came back from work, had an argument with his wife, and murdered her and his children. He knew exactly what he had done but did not feel any remorse or pity over it. He knew that he had to hide their bodies. He had to make himself unsuspectable.

. . .

He buried the bodies miles away from his home in the deep forests that lined the mountain. He felt free.

At first glance, Todd seems to be evil. He killed his wife and children and then buried their bodies to hide his infraction. He was calculated and cold in the aftermath of the incident.

Let's compare Todd and Alan. Alan was a drunken man who killed his wife and felt horrible over it. Todd is a man who killed his wife and children and was cold enough to get himself out of the situation. Are both men evil? Are both of them the same? If not, which of them is evil? Who is more evil?

The short answer is that both of them are evil. The difference between them is that Todd did deliberate harm to his family, while Alan did not. It is evident from Alan's actions that he did not plan the kill at all. Therefore, his actions may be excusable on moral grounds as an unavoidable accident or unforeseeable contingency. However, he is *not* excused of manslaughter.

TODD, on the other hand, caused deliberate harm to his family. He was cold and calculated in the aftermath of the murder. In the throes of his anger or ill will, he did excessive harm to his family and lacked an excuse as to why he did it. Therefore, Todd's actions are inexcusable.

THESE EXAMPLES SHOW that evil comes in different degrees. One man has evidently committed a wrongdoing, and is agonizing over it; whereas the other has deliberately committed a wrongdoing (he was not under any duress or influence), and his response is to hide it. The latter's response to his actions makes him seem evil, whereas the former's response makes him pitiable. It does not free him of his crime, but it does make his action seem less evil at first glance.

THEREFORE, it is evident that there is a difference between the severity of evil actions. An inexcusable or deliberate evil action is categorized by the absence of morality, whereas an excusable evil action or wrongdoing is not absent of morality. This shows that an essential property of evil actions is intent. If the evildoer means to harm their victim significantly, then they are committing an evil action. If a person did not mean to do their victim any harm, but it did happen, then they may be morally excused for their actions.

In simple words, the main difference between the severity of evil acts is intent.

What is Evil?

In simple terms, evil actions are actions that have a very high moral significance. They are characterized as 'wrong' or 'bad' or 'horrifying'. According to John Kekes, Evil "... involves serious harm that causes fatal or lasting physical injury, as do, for instance, murder, torture, and mutilation." Evil actions violate their victims' physical security and go against fundamental moral prohibitions that protect human well-being.

To be truly evil, a person must have sought to do harm to someone by planning to commit some morally wrong action with no prompting from any other person (the success of this endeavor is not to be taken into account when categorizing someone as evil). The person must have carried out their plan with the intention of causing harm to others either psychologically or physically.

When asked to analyze their actions, these evil individuals will either deny that their actions were morally wrong, be incoherent (make no logical sense), or show indifference. Some great examples of evil people are Ted Bundy and Adolf Hitler. One was a serial killer, and the other was a mass murderer. One was motivated by rejection, and the other by making his race pure.

We can label someone 'evil' when they have participated in various atrocities and horrors, such as terrorist attacks, mass murders, torture, killing sprees, and genocides. These are actions that defy moral understanding and are so convoluted that they are hard to understand.

THIS MEANS that for any action to be characterized as "evil" moral agency must be absent from that action. In other words, an action has to be morally wrong to be characterized as evil action. Do moral wrongdoings make an action evil? Let's take the case of a man who lied to his wife when he told her that he was at work when in reality he was going to buy a gift for her birthday. Is he an evil person just because he told a lie? Is he evil because he lied to his wife?

LET'S TAKE ANOTHER EXAMPLE. A father killed the man who raped his daughter. After killing the man, the father went to the police and surrendered himself into their custody. Is he evil? Does the murder of the man who raped his daughter make him evil? What if this man was an executioner with the support of the law behind him? Would he be evil then?

. . .

THIS RAISES THE QUESTION: how can you classify evil exactly? If a man isn't evil when he lies to his wife or when he kills a rapist, then what is evil exactly? When evil actions come in degrees of severity, identifying true 'evil' becomes hard. "Evil" is a term used for actions that defy moral understanding. "Wrongness" has been used as a term to describe things that are uncomfortable or unusual. This means that "wrong" actions are very different from 'evil' actions.

THEREFORE, LABELING SOMETHING AS 'EVIL' requires the person to commit extreme morally despicable acts. The acts must cause serious harm to their victim and lack excuse or moral agents such as honesty, mercy, etc.

There are two concepts of evil: a broad concept and a narrow concept. The broad concept states that any wrongful action, character flaw, or bad experience is "evil". This evil results from the negligence of moral agents such as mercy or kindness. Murder and lying are examples of such evils. In the broad sense, evil is a theological concept. It is related to religion and the sense of good and evil. A man is labeled as "good" if he commits certain acts such as giving alms, respecting others, and being kind, while a man is labeled as "bad" if he commits certain acts such as vigilante justice, murder, rape, and compulsive lying. In this view, every action that is deemed 'bad' is characterized as 'evil'.

The narrow concept of evil, on the other hand, only categorizes the most morally despicable acts, people, or events as 'evil'. In this concept, the term 'evil' is used as the worst possible condemnation and denigration imaginable. Moral agents are very prevalent in this concept; therefore, moral condemnations of the evil act, person, or event to an extreme extent is possible. This view states that if human beings are moral agents—they ascribe to morals such as respect, kindness, or mercy —*then only they can perform evil actions.* Usually, the narrow sense of evil is used to characterize evil actions in moral, political, and legal contexts.

Evil and Will

Immanuel Kant, in his *Religion Within the Limits of Reason Alone,* stated that a person is only morally good if they choose to perform morally right actions *because* they are morally right. Not for any other reason. He claims that anyone who does not have a morally good will has an evil will.

Furthermore, he states that there are three different degrees of corrupted will. The first degree is a frail will. A person with a frail will try to perform morally right actions because they are morally right. However, the frail-willed person does not actually manage to perform these actions. This person instead performs wrongs due to their weak will. An example would be a person who vows that they will stop lying but does not follow through due to weakness of will. They do not have the power to force themselves not to lie.

THE SECOND STAGE of corruption is impurity. A person at this stage does not perform morally right actions because they are morally right. Rather, this person performs them partly because of some incentive such as self-interest and partly because these actions are morally right. An example could be a person who tells the truth only because of the trustworthiness they can cultivate. They do not do it because it is morally right; they do it because it is in their best interests to do so (they see the benefits of being truthful).

IN THE LAST STAGE, the corruption of will is complete. At this stage, will is perverse or wicked. The person with a perverse will prioritize themselves over moral law, only conforming to the moral law if it lines up with their interests. Kant argues that this type of will is the worst form of evil. This person doesn't have to do anything wrong to be considered evil. They *are* evil just because they prioritize themselves over moral laws.

THIS RAISES AN IMPORTANT QUESTION: is a person who prioritizes themselves over moral laws an evil person, even if they commit no wrongs?

MOST THEORISTS such as Kekes and Garrard disagree with Kant's view. They do not believe that prioritizing self-interest over the moral law makes people evil. They say that the evilness of a person or their will depends on their motives and the harm they bring about. In other words, they believe that the harm that a person brings to others around themselves dictates how evil they are.

FOR EXAMPLE, how is a sadistic torturer different from a person who speaks the truth to gain something? The former indicates an evil psyche, while the latter shows an individual lacking in moral goodness. If Kant's view were taken into account, then the person who spoke the truth would also be regarded as evil because he prized self-interest over moral laws.

PAUL FORMOSA ARGUES that Kant's views are correct because they suggest that even the best of us can revert to evil, and therefore, should always be vigilant against the radical evil of our natures.

THERE ARE many contradicting views of evil and weakness of will shared by theorists all over the world. Some theorists argue that a weak will leads to evil, while other theorists argue that it is the intention to do evil that makes an action evil. This means that corruption or weakness of will are not good indicators of whether a person is evil or not. It is the intention of the person which determines if they are evil or not.

Theories of Evil Action

There are dozens of theories put forward by dozens of theorists about the conditions necessary for an act to be deemed evil. Some theorists believe that evil character is the root cause of evil. In simple words, they essentially believe that only an evil person is capable of evil acts. Other theorists believe that evil action is the root of evil. They believe that a person who is prone to evil actions is evil. Their character does not make them evil, rather their actions do.

These conflicting views muddy the definition of evil even further. Is a person who commits evil morally corrupt, or is their character corrupt?

Evil and Harm

Most theorists believe that for an action to be categorized as evil at least one victim must have been significantly harmed. John Kekes, *In the Roots of Evil,* states that the effect or harm of evil must be serious and excessive. He specifies that serious harm that which "interferes with the functioning of a person as a full-fledged agent". This means that the harm caused must make it hard for the victim to behave like they did before they were harmed. Claudia Card argues that the harm of evil must be intolerable —harm that makes life not worth living from the victim's point of view. In this view, for an action to be classified as evil, significant harm has to be inflicted on the victim.

According to this view, an action is only evil if it causes devastating effects or significant harm to the victim. For example, a person who rapes another person is evil because they have caused significant harm to their victim.

However, a few arguments have been used to counter this belief.

Some theorists argue that an evil action does not have to cause significant harm to the victim to be characterized as evil. They believe that humans can perform evil actions by *attempting* to cause harm. This means that the person does not have to succeed in doing any harm. Their intention to cause harm is enough to make them an evil person. For example, in this view, a person who tries to murder someone but does not succeed (for whatever reason) will still be characterized as an evil person, regardless of their success or failure.

OTHER THEORISTS ARGUE that a person does not have to directly inflict or allow harm to be labeled as evil if they take pleasure in a victim's suffering. For example, in this view, a man named Hilton takes pleasure in witnessing his brother's downfall. Although he has not caused his brother's downfall, he still enjoys the spectacle. This act of sadistic voyeurism doesn't cause any harm to the victim directly. So, maybe it couldnot be classified as an evil act.

HOWEVER, Paul Formosa argues that sadistic voyeurism is an evil action because the voyeur allows harm to occur to the victim. Therefore, they take part in the victim's suffering. This means that if someone took pleasure in witnessing a victim being harmed, then they would have committed an evil act, whether they directly caused harm to the victim or not.

THIS VIEW STATES that evil actions need not cause much harm to the victim in order to be labeled as such. It tells us that sadistic voyeurs through their intentions, motives, and feelings, can be characterized as evil individuals even though they didn't perform evil actions.

THEREFORE, assuming that harm is an essential component of evil, the question that arises is: how much harm is required for an action to be regarded as evil? Is it necessary to cause harm in order to commit evil?

ALL THESE CONFLICTING theories only agree on one thing: suffering is caused by harm. Some theories suggest that immense levels of harm make an action evil, while others argue that almost no harm is required to characterize an action as evil. This means that some level of harm is essential for an act to be deemed evil.

. . .

Conclusion.

There seems to be a direct correlation between harm and evil in the eyes of many theorists. For many, harm is an essential component of evil actions. For an action to be recognized as evil, some form of harm must have occurred; the severity of harm directly influences the severity of an evil action.

Therefore, an evil action is only labeled as such if there is some harm caused to the victim.

3

GOOD VS. BAD: IS HUMANITY DOOMED SINCE ITS INCEPTION?

"In each of us, two natures are at war – the good and the evil. All our lives the fight goes on between them and one of them must conquer. But in our own hands lies the power to choose – what we want most to be we are."

— Robert Louis Stevenson

The Myth of Gyges.

Plato, in his *Republic,* argues about the difference between man's predilection towards evil and good. In the *Myth of Gyges,* he conducts a thought experiment by repeating a myth that questions a man's commitment to justice, to balance, and to good.

The myth goes something like this: a long time ago, a shepherd named Gyges was in the service of the king of Lydia. One day when Gyges was feeding his flock, the earth shook mightily and was torn asunder. A tunnel had opened in the earth so deep that Gyges couldn't glean its depths. Gyges, astonished and curious, stepped down into the tunnel. He saw many marvels in the chamber underneath the earth, including a statue of a horse in which lay a dead body, seemingly more than human, wearing a golden ring.

Gyges, awed and shocked, took the ring and ascended back to his flock. Sometime later, the day came when all the shepherds gathered together to send their monthly report to the king. Gyges sat in the assembly and accidentally turned the collet—the part where the stone in a ring is put in—of his gold ring outward.

He became invisible.

HIS BRETHREN STARTED TALKING over him as if he were not present near them at all. He was astonished. So, he tried again and again—all to the same effect. Then he began to wonder... What else could he do with the ring?

MANY, many things, he realized. After coming to this realization, Gyges decided to go to the capital of the king. He contrived to be chosen as one of the messengers who took the shepherd's reports to the crown. As soon as he arrived in the capital, he seduced the queen and with her help slew the king, and took the kingdom as his own.

PLATO GOES FURTHER and elaborates the consequences of all people having this kind of power. He says that, "No man would keep his hands off what was not his own when he could safely take what he liked out of the market… or kill or release from prison whom he would, and in respects be like a God among men." He essentially claims that all men have the capacity to be evil—to be unjust. He says that if a man can get away with being unjust then he will be unjust, no matter what.

BUT IS THIS TRUE? Is man truly inclined towards bad? If we all had an invisible ring, would we also commit the crime that Gyges committed? Would we still commit evil if there were no one to see us?

Are we truly, as humans, inherently bad?

THESE ARE ALL GOOD QUESTIONS, the answers to which have been much argued over since antiquity.

THERE HAS BEEN a debate raging on for hundreds of years among philosophers, theologists, scholars, and priests over whether humans are fundamentally good or evil. The debate earnestly started when 17th and 18thcentury philosophers Jean-Jacques Rousseau and Thomas Hobbes put forward opposite theories of human nature. Hobbes held the view that human nature was inherently "solitary, poor, nasty, brutish, and short," while Rousseau believed that human nature was good, it was civilization that turned us evil.

HOBBES BELIEVED that humanity was inherently self-interested and looked out for itself first and foremost. He believed that our self-interest and our desire for social standing drove us into conflict with each other. He saw lasting peace or goodness as a rare and fragile achievement, something that was immensely hard to attain because we, as humans, were naturally predisposed to doing what was best for us regardless of whether it broke moral laws.

. . .

Rousseau, on the other hand, believed that humanity was inherently good but that we were corrupted by industrialization and the inequality produced by economic progress. He believed that inequality bred social division, and it was this that led us to become evil. He thought that once corrupted, the chances for redemption for us became vanishingly slight.

Is Rousseau right in saying that humans are born pure and only corrupted by social institutions? Or, is Thomas Hobbes right in saying that humans are born with the capacity to do great evil? Does an evil man have no capacity for good? Or does a good man not have the capacity for evil?

Both of these positions have merit. There have been countless examples of men and women throughout history who committed great acts of both good and evil. Stories passed down through generations reiterate the tales of men and women who, with their courage and bravery, fought and died for their ideals and their people. The most famous of these people was Jesus, a Jewish messiah who fought for his ideals and was martyred for standing up to his oppressors.

Other examples of people who had a profound effect on the lives of others are Nelson Mandela, the man who fought for voting rights for black people in South Africa and was jailed for it; Mahatma Gandhi, a peaceful and religiously tolerant man who led the Indian people to independence; Martin Luther King, an American Baptist minister who fought for equality and human rights for African American and economically disadvantaged people, and all victims of injustice, and Malcom X, an African American Muslim minister and a human rights activist who fought for the right of self-determination for black people in the USA.

Something all of these activists had in common was that all of them were jailed for voicing their opinions. Mandela was incarcerated for 27 years in prison for trying to overthrow the ghastly apartheid rule in South Africa. Martin Luther King, Mahatma Gandhi, and Malcom X were all assassinated because they fought for something that the people at that time were not willing to give.

These examples tell us that there were people in the world who did incredible good. They changed the lives of generations to come. They fought for justice, rights, and equality. They became the spokespeople of those who couldn't fight for themselves.

Were they born good? Were they inherently good? Did they not have a shred of evil in their bodies?

Let's take the example of Martin Luther King, a man so admired that he is nearly regarded as a saint. Martin Luther King, the Baptist minister who was a champion for oppressed people, was accused of infidelity by the FBI. The agency had started tapping into King's phones in the spring or summer of 1963 because they were worried about communist infiltration by some of King's allies. Instead of finding communist plotting, the FBI became spectators to King's near constant sexual activities with countless women as he traveled on the road. Later, some recorded FBI tapes even revealed that Martin had encouraged the rape of a woman by his own compatriot.

THIS DOES NOT SEEM like the best of behaviors for a "good" person, does it? But, let's go through another example before making a verdict.

MAHATMA GANDHI, the man who led India to independence, was actually anti-black and believed that black people were beneath Indian people. He even supported the British during the Zulu rebellion and actively encouraged British retaliation. He was also a misogynist and a sexual predator. He tested his vow of celibacy by conducting "experiments", which involved him putting himself in predatory closeness with women, both young and old, in his Ashram. He even included his grand-niece in these experiments. At a time of intense Hindu-Muslim violence in Bengal, he asked her to sleep with him unclothed in his bed as "the ultimate test" of both their purities. Gandhi continued these "experiments" until his death. Young women were seen crying or laughing hysterically after going through these "experiments" with him.

Some of the "experiments" Gandhi did were frankly horrifying. How could a man so revered commit these actions? Was the error of his ways not evident to him? Did he not care about the effect he would have on these women?

The people presented in these examples had a massive impact on millions of people. They held the torch to a better future. They were regarded as essentially "good" people. This regard makes their actions all the more horrifying.

This sentiment brings to mind a question: if these "saints" were inherently good, how could they commit such crimes? How could they vacillate between good and evil so easily?

. . .

Unless... they *were not* born good. Could it be that instead of being inherently good, they were both inherently good *and* evil? It is not a stretch of imagination to picture that, is it?

So, is man capable of great good and great evil at the same time?

So far we have only discussed the nature of good men and their "dark side". Now, let's move on to some of the most hated men in the world and see if they had as dual a nature as these "good" men.

Let's take the example of Adolf Hitler, the Fuhrer of the Third Reich. A man so evil that even decades after his death, he is despised all over the world.

Was he born evil, or was he born good?

. . .

ADOLF HITLER, the man who killed over six million people, was *notoriously kind and courteous* to his personal staff and considered very *likable* and *approachable* by them. His secretary, Traudl Junge, described him as "a pleasant boss and a fatherly friend." It is said that he loved young children and dogs. He was also vegetarian because he despised animal cruelty.

HITLER WENT from an aspiring artist to a brutal dictator. He instigated the deaths of millions of people through his ideologies. He launched a crusade against Jewish people that ended with over 6 million of them losing their lives. Was he born good or evil? By all accounts he seems like a pleasant person. If he was born evil, how is it that he committed good?

HOW IS it that he had the capacity for both great evil and good?

TED BUNDY, a notorious serial killer who killed and raped over 30 women, was considered charming and enigmatic by the people who met him. Bundy's friend Marlin Lee Vortman once said of him, “He was the kind of guy you’d want your sister to marry.”

In reality, Ted Bundy was an evil person. He deliberately harmed innocent women. He performed grotesque acts on their dead bodies. When helping profile a killer, he famously claimed that, “Women are possessions… Women are merchandise.”

How is it that Ted Bundy despite being such a good person to everyone, raped and killed women? How is it that he had another side that was admired by his colleagues?

How is it that Hitler and Ted Bundy, both regarded as incredibly evil, showed goodness? Were their natures good, but their actions evil? Or, was it the opposite? How is it that humanity shows such duality of nature?

Noel Coward captured the strangeness of this duality perfectly. He said, "It is hard to imagine, considering the inherent silliness, cruelty, and superstition of the human race, how it has contrived to last as long as it has. The witch-hunting, the torturing, the gullibility, the massacres, the intolerance, the wild futility of human behavior over the centuries is hardly credible."

His view seems credible. How often has humanity fallen into a quagmire of evil so deep that it struggled to get out? How often have we committed obscenities in the name of good?

Yet, how is it that most of the time we do wonderful things that are completely opposite to these evils? We are kind, reasonable, and cooperative. We work together, show tolerance, trust, and understanding.

How is it that we are capable of this perplexing combination of moral tendencies? How can we be the nastiest of people and also the nicest?

THE GREAT ODDITY about humanity is the way we vacillate from heartbreaking generosity to great tyranny. If we were born to be good, how is it that we commit such vile acts that burn through the pages of history? If we were born to be evil, how is it that saints who died to keep their people safe exist?

THIS CONUNDRUM HAS PIQUED the interest of philosophers throughout the existence of humanity. When we look back ten thousand years and riffle through archeologists records, we find that our hunter-gatherer ancestors shared food, helped the needy, and were tolerant and peaceful. Yet at the same time, evidence also indicates that these same people were raiders, torturers, executors, and were as cruel as the great tyrants of our age. Their capacity for great violence and great kindness was not dissimilar to what is exhibited by all humanity today.

. . .

THEY WERE JUST LIKE US. They had the same capacity for violence and kindness as exhibited by Hitler and Bundy. They also showed the same corrupted goodness shown by Gandhi and by King. Some of them were drawn more towards the dark side or were selfish, while others were drawn more towards the good and were selfless.

THE TWO CLASSICAL EXPLANATIONS—PRESENTED by Hobbes and Rousseau—for this paradoxical combination of selfishness and selflessness both assume that our social behavior is determined by our biology, or how we were born. Rousseau posits that humanity is inherently good, that our potential for corruption stands in the way of peace. He says that we are born good but are susceptible to corruption.

HOBBES, on the other hand, claims that we are inherently bad. That we are born selfish and competitive and have such destructive potential that were it not curbed by civilizing forces; would destroy everything around us.

. . .

Both these views are correct. We are naturally good in the way that Rousseau is said to have claimed, and we are naturally selfish, much as Hobbes argued. The potential for good and evil resides in every individual. Our goodness can be heightened or corrupted by our actions, just as our selfishness can be magnified or diminished by our actions. Thus, it seems humans have the same propensity for both wickedness and kindness.

"A Native American elder once described his own inner struggles in this manner: Inside of me, there are two dogs. One of the dogs is mean and evil. The other dog is good. The mean dog fights the good dog all the time. When asked which dog wins, he reflected for a moment and replied, the one I feed the most."

— George Bernard Shaw

Throughout the history of mankind, countless evil men and women have committed good acts, and countless good men and women have committed evil acts. This curious tale of the duality of human nature has been recorded untold times in the annals of history. Therefore, the argument that a man is inherently evil or good is debatable because there is no way to know if a person is predestined to be evil or good.

So, in itself, by nature, humanity is not evil or good. We are instead a puzzling mix of both for we have the potential to be both evil and good. We can either be selfish—as the myth of Gyges shows—or we can be selfless as countless men and women have been throughout history.

4

NATURE VS. NURTURE: WHAT MAKES US EVIL?

"He who fights with monsters might take care lest he thereby become a monster. And if you gaze for long into an abyss, the abyss gazes also into you."

— Friedrich Nietzsche, Beyond Good and Evil

EVIL IS A CONCEPT THAT IS APPLIED TO THOSE individuals who commit actions that do terrible harm to others. In other words, evil is essentially excessive harm that is done by human beings to other human beings.

. . .

The savage horrors done by humanity have rarely varied in ages past: massacres, mass starvations, imprisonments, torture, death, maiming and mutilation in war, tyranny, and humiliation. From holy wars to honor killings, all these evils have stayed constant and undeniable throughout the centuries.

Sometimes necessity demands that evil be done. We believe that if evil is done unknowingly and unintentionally, it is excusable. But often evil is done by people who know what they are doing, mean to do it, and don't do it in order to prevent greater evil. These are genuine, inexcusable evil actions.

These evildoers know that they are harming people. They also know that their actions go against every established moral principle in their society. They are aware of these moral tenants, but they coldly and deliberately choose to do evil without feeling any regret. Maybe they are indifferent to the plight of the people they harm, or if they are not indifferent then the concern they have for their victims is outweighed by some other consideration they grant far more importance.

Politicians who lie to gain their office, young men who rob the elderly of their savings, street gangs who terrorize people for money, friends who expose confidential information entrusted to them, businessmen who sell spoiled products or products that they know will harm people are just some examples of many people who commit evil actions to achieve their goals.

Some examples of these evil actions are romanticized and looked over. Some are looked over because they are familiar and common, others because they were excusable. But by whatever reason an evil action is excused, it is *not* rendered good at all. These evil actions were not motivated by altruism, rather they were motivated by either selfishness, malice, jealousy, aggression, greed, prejudice, or hostility. There were no grand passions that fueled these evil actions. Rather there is shrewd and ruthless calculation of what the victims can bear done by the evildoer before they set out to complete their task.

There are multitudes of explanations offered by dozens of reputed scholars such as Plato, Augustine, Hobbes, Butler, Kant, Bradley, and Leibniz, among many others, which have tried to answer the questions of what causes evil and why there is so much of it. Their explanations go over many factors such as psychology, biology of human nature, and societal forces that influence human behavior.

IN THE PREVIOUS CHAPTER, we came to the conclusion that humanity is capable of both evil and good, that we inherently carry the potential to be both evil and good. So, what causes us to commit evil? Do societal forces such as inequality or social division lead us to commit evil actions? Or, do psychological or biological factors?

SUPPOSED Causes of Evil

THERE ARE many different reasons why people commit evil actions. Most explanations try to justify evil actions by giving examples of human action. The main difference between these explanations is whether they locate the causes of human action within the evildoers or in conditions outside them. Internal causes are psychological, such as cruelty, ignorance, or malice. External causes are natural influences such as injustice, inequality, social division or more.

According to John Kekes, the causes of evil actions can also be active or passive. Active causes make evildoers commit evil actions. These causes can be internal or psychological such as calculation, desire, jealousy, or malice. They can also be religious, ideological, or economic external influences. The crimes that the crusaders committed in their Holy war against Christian heretics and all who helped them can be taken as active causes of evil.

The causes of evil actions are passive if "evil actions are the result of either something evildoers lack, such as reason, knowledge, or self-control, or the absence of external limits, like moral prohibitions or strict laws." John Kekes, The Roots of Evil.

Thus, an active cause *makes* the evildoer commit an evil action, whereas a passive cause *allows* them to do it or have it happen in front of them. Both the evildoer's actions and inactions cause serious, excessive, and inexcusable harm to others.

Internal Causes of Evil Actions

The internal causes of evil actions stem from psychological factors such as jealousy, anger, hatred, revenge, malice, ignorance, neglect, psychological trauma, megalomania, and ignorance, among many others. From these psychological factors can stem massacres, genocides, mass starvations, mass murder, spree killings, and much more.

Such was the case with Maximilien Robespierre, the monster who killed thousands of innocents in the French Revolution, and the megalomaniac who fervently believed that reason and morality were at his side—that he knew best.

He is quoted as saying, "There do exist pure and sensitive souls... You can feel it, at this moment, burning in your hearts; I can feel it in my own." Robespierre believed that since the people of France had been corrupted, they could not be trusted to know what was best for them, but he, Robespierre, knew, because he was uncorrupted.

He regarded it as his duty to make sure the corrupted population would live according to what he knew best because he was pure. He convinced others that his will was the will of the population, that if everyone acted on it, they would be as pure as he was. Many followed him not because they were convinced by his ideologies, but because he let them act on their worst urges, which they had to hide when order and law prevailed.

Others wanted to understand what was going on and wanted justification for the atrocities committed by Robespierre and his people. So, when Robespierre gave his explanation that, "There are only two parties in France: the people and its enemies. We must exterminate those miserable villains who are eternally conspiring against the rights of man... We must exterminate all our enemies." they believed him not because they were convinced, but because they had to find some way to balance the atrocities they saw committed. Fear of Robespierre played a part in silencing any opposition.

SCHAMA RECOUNTS THAT ROBESPIERRE, "rejoiced that 'a river of blood would now divide France from its enemies.'" In essence, he gave the dissatisfied people of France the permission to finally satisfy their worst urges once and for all.

HE UNLEASHED the Terror on France, mostly on Paris, the center of the Revolution. The mob in Paris was mostly made of *sans-culottes* ("without breeches")—men and women who supported themselves through prostitution, begging, crime, and other odd jobs that nobody would take on. The mob's resentment for those in power boiled over and Robespierre took full advantage.

STANLEY LOOMIS WRITES in *Paris in the Terror* that, in the massacres performed in September

1792, "the bloody work went on for five . . . days and nights. On the morning of the third, the prison of La Force was entered and here took place the murder of the Princesse de Lamballe... The frenzy of the crazed and drunken murderers appears to have reached its highest pitch at La Force. Cannibalism, disembowelment and acts of indescribable ferocity took place here. The Princess . . . refused to swear her hatred of the King and Queen and was duly handed over to the mob. She was dispatched with a pike thrust, her still beating heart was ripped from her body and devoured, her legs and arms were severed from her body and shot through cannon. The horrors that were then perpetrated on her disemboweled torso are indescribable... It has been loosely assumed . . . that most of the other victims were, like herself, aristocrats—an assumption that for some curious reason is often supposed to mitigate these crimes. Very few victims were, in fact, of the former nobility—less than thirty out of the fifteen hundred who were killed."

After securing Paris in 1793, Robespierre appointed commissioners to enforce the tenants of his Revolution outside the capital. In the city of Lyon, they started executing the "enemies" of the Republic; however, soon guillotining was found to be a messy way of culling the ranks of "political garbage". So, they found another way. Simon Schama in *Citizen* writes that, "A number of the condemned, then, were executed in mass shootings… As many as sixty prisoners were tied in a line by ropes and shot at with cannon. Those who were not killed outright by the fire were finished off with sabers, bayonets, and rifles… By the time that the killings… had finished, one thousand nine hundred and five people had met their end." The commissioner in Nantes "supplemented the guillotine with… 'vertical deportations.'… Holes were punched in the sides of… barges… Prisoners were put in with their hands and feet tied and the boats pushed into the center of the river… The victims helplessly watched the water rise about them… Prisoners were stripped of their clothes and belongings… Young men and women were tied naked together in the boats. Estimates of those who perished in this manner vary greatly, but there were certainly no fewer than two thousand."

. . .

WHEN ASKED to comment on an execution of a man, Robespierre said: "Even if he had been innocent he had to be condemned if his death could be useful." He showed that he held no remorse for the crimes he was committing. He showed that he only cared for his ends.

SCHAMA FURTHER RECOUNTS of the Vendéan massacre that, "Every atrocity the time could imagine was meted out to the defenseless population. Women were routinely raped, children killed, both mutilated… At Gonnord… two hundred old people, along with mothers and children, were forced to kneel in front of a large pit they had dug; they were then shot so as to tumble into their own grave… Thirty children and two women were buried alive when earth was shoveled onto the pit."

MOST OF THE people who were killed in these horrifying instances were innocent of all crimes that had been leveled against them.

ROBESPIERRE UNLOOSED the most depraved urges of society's dregs on the people of France and was unapologetic when he saw the disaster that enfolded because the resulting anarchy served his purpose—to frighten his opponents into submission and to establish himself firmly in power.

He encouraged the mob in Paris to go about their horrifying way by saying, "We must exterminate all our enemies with the law in our hands." His closest ally Saint-Just even said that, "The republic consists in the extermination of everything that opposes it."

Robespierre's belief that he knew best had him commit the worst atrocities imaginable. He was not ignorant of the impact of his actions, in fact, he even lauded the Revolutionaries for their actions and encouraged them to do their worst.

He wanted the world to be like he envisioned it, and when he found that people disagreed, he had them killed. He ordered the murder of thousands of people just because he *suspected* that they might not agree with his passionate views.

. . .

HIS REGIME WAS JUST like the countless murderous regimes who claimed that their aim was to find lasting peace, but that their wicked enemies—corrupted in their nature—conspired against them and threatened their achievements. The same corrupted regimes which claimed that the threat from these enemies was so serious that extreme measures had to be taken to exterminate them, that once the grave threat was averted, the extreme measures would no longer be necessary.

AND HIS PEOPLE BELIEVED THAT. They believed that lynching, mutilating, drowning, disemboweling, and burying their victims alive was only a means to an end. That it was all in the name of good.

ROBESPIERRE WAS NOT IGNORANT, nor was he indoctrinated to believe a single point-of-view. He was a lawyer and had the capacity to sift through evidence and evaluate for himself the facts that were presented to him. Therefore, the only conclusion that comes to mind is that he knew absolutely what he was doing... He knew that his actions would cause havoc, and he was not the least bit remorseful about it.

MAXIMILIAN ROBESPIERRE CONDEMNED thousands of people to death, simply because he thought he knew best.

THEREFORE, if evil is serious, excessive, and morally inexcusable harm caused by human beings, then what was done to the people of France by Maximillian Robespierre was pure evil.

EXTERNAL CAUSES of Evil Actions

> The line between good and evil is permeable and almost anyone can be induced to cross it when pressured by situational forces.
>
> —Philip Zimbardo

External causes of evil act upon a human being from the outside. They are societal forces such as injustice, inequality, social division, economic influences, or more that lead human beings to evil actions.

From 1886-1908, an incredible number of atrocities were committed in the Congo Free State, a colony under the rule of Belgium King Leopold II. Unmet quotas were the main reason behind the retribution. The boom in demand for natural rubber made the colony a gold mine. Acres of land were granted to private companies by the Crown so they could extract and export rubber.

Since the private companies had been given full power over the people living on their lands (they could use any measure to increase production), forced labor and violent coercion were used to collect rubber cheaply, all to maximize profit. A labor policy—called the "Red Rubber system" by critics—was introduced in 1891 that demanded forced labor as a form of taxation. This essentially created a slave society where workers were forced to collect rubber in order to survive.

At first, the rubber quotas were being met, but soon the Congo natives were overworked and could not produce as much rubber. The quotas were usually set without any regard for the welfare of the workers and without consideration of the number of workers. So, many workers were overworked. It is no wonder that production began to decline.

Violent coercion such as beatings and whippings was used as a way to force workers to extract rubber. Hostages were taken from villages to ensure the collection and delivery of rubber. These hostages could be men, women, children, elders and even the chieftains themselves. Entire villages which disobeyed the forced labor law were destroyed in retaliation.

One junior officer described the raid that was done to punish a village that had protested against the forced labor policy. He said that the commanding officer, "ordered [them] to cut off the heads of the men and hang them on the village palisades ... and to hang the women and the children on the palisade in the form of a cross."

The Force Publique—a military force of black and white men—enforced rubber production in Congo. The Force Publique's directive was to make sure that rubber production ran smoothly. If a slave failed to meet the rubber collection quotas, they were shot to death by the Force Publique. Since it was widely believed that these officers would use the munitions issued to them for hunting or mutiny, every officer who killed a worker was to present a severed hand as proof.

A Danish missionary after seeing a Congolese person killed for the first time wrote that a soldier who had seen his horror said to him, "'Don't take this to heart so much. They kill us if we don't bring the rubber. The Commissioner has promised us if we have plenty of hands he will shorten our service."

. . .

As a result, severed hands were used to pay off rubber quotas. Soldiers would come and collect the hands of people to pay off the rubber quotas. The situation got so bad that whole villages severed the hands of their people in order to fill the unrealistic quotas.

Peter Forbrath in *The River Congo: The Discovery, Exploration, and Exploitation of the World's Most Dramatic Rivers* said that, "The baskets of severed hands, set down at the feet of the European post commanders, became the symbol of the Congo Free State. ... The collection of hands became an end in itself. *Force Publique* soldiers brought them to the stations in place of rubber; they even went out to harvest them instead of rubber ... They became a sort of currency. They came to be used to make up for shortfalls in rubber quotas, to replace ... the people who were demanded for the forced labor gangs; and the *Force Publique* soldiers were paid their bonuses on the basis of how many hands they collected."

Companies such as ABIR put Congolese people who resisted into forced labor camps. Others outright killed anyone who opposed them. Hostages were taken to ensure that quotas were met. Workers were mutilated in order to fill the rubber quotas. Congolese men and women were essentially enslaved. All these atrocities were committed in the name of economic interests.

SOLDIERS WHO WORKED in the Congo believed that their lives were better than the Congolese people. It was better that they lived instead of the Congolese people. Every soldier who refused to do the ghastly task of severing hands was killed. So, soldiers learned to prize themselves over anybody else. After all, forced labor was cheap, soldiers were not.

THE RUBBER COLLECTING companies did not care at all for the Congolese people. They cared for their profit margins and nothing else. Even in Belgium, King Leopold did not care. He famously said, "Cut off hands—that's idiotic. I'd cut off all the rest of them, but not hands. That's the one thing I need in the Congo." This showed that he didn't mind that the workers were mutilated; he just minded that the part that he needed most—to work his fields—was cut off.

ECONOMIC INFLUENCES DROVE THESE COMPANIES, the Force Publique, and King Leopold II to commit heinous crimes against the people of the Congo. They harmed and killed millions of Congolese people, all in their hunger for profit.

5

THE FUNDAMENTAL ASPECTS OF BEING EVIL: HOW DO YOU KNOW?

> "Evil acts are done by human beings, and it is within them that their causes are sought."
>
> —John Kekes.

EVIL ACTIONS CAUSE EXCESSIVE AND SERIOUS harm to their victims. They are done by human beings to other human beings. Social conditions can exacerbate or diminish the potential for evil acts within individuals, but they are not sufficient to explain them. Many times, only some of the people living under the same conditions—poverty, injustice, etc.—become evildoers. Similarly, at times, two like evil acts could be done under very different social conditions.

LET'S take the example of Janelle who has lived through poverty, hunger, and suffering. She wept when she saw men and women die before her eyes without her being able to do anything. When she grew up and worked hard, she became a doctor, not because she aspired to be one, but because she wanted to help people.

MICAH, on the other hand, went through the same poverty, hunger, and suffering Janelle did. They both lived in the same camp. He watched, unable to help, as his friends died. He got angry at the establishment. He knew that this was their fault. So, he started to work against them. He robbed them because they robbed him of his friends. He killed them because they deserved it. He murdered hundreds of innocents just because they lived within that establishment, and he cheered his people on when they murdered the innocent.

. . .

THERE IS a vast difference between Janelle and Micah's choices. They both went through the same things, but they both had different reactions to them. Janelle saved countless lives; Micah took countless lives. These examples show that social conditions have the ability to heighten or alleviate evil acts, but they cannot explain them. Only through psychological factors can we explain evil actions and where they stemmed from.

IT IS hard to accept that the causes of evil are within,, not outside us. It is hard to accept that in doing evil we express a deep part of ourselves because this acceptance destroys any illusion or hopes we hold about ourself and others.

IN THIS CHAPTER we will focus on the common qualities shown by men and women who committed evil acts throughout history. We will focus on the common characteristics shown by evil people.

Evil, Be Thou My Good

First of all, evil is primarily serious harm that is caused by human beings to other human beings. This harm is inexcusable on any moral grounds. Any ideology that leads a person to commit massacres, spree killings, genocides, mass murder, extermination, and imprisonment, among others, is considered evil.

In the previous chapters, it has been established that man has the potential for both good and evil, therefore, if we succeed in preventing the expression of one side in one way, then it may be expressed in another. This is why evil is a permanent adversity that plagues humankind and coping with it is extremely difficult. Using reason to resist evil does not work many times. Not only does reason favor good, but it also favors evil actions, depending on our character and the circumstances we find ourselves in.

. . .

Evildoers cause more harm than they need to in order to achieve their goals. They are motivated by malevolence and so treat their victims with ill will, hatred, or rage. This can be shown through the sheer quantity of the harm they do, such as the murder of thousands of innocent victims, or by the quality of their actions, such as torturing children. They don't just break moral laws; they flaunt their contempt for moral laws.

All these components have ranges: malevolent motives can range from short-term rage to lifelong hatred; harm can range from torture of one person—physical or mental—to the torture of thousands; and inexcusable moral actions can range from culpable ignorance to knowingly doing evil for evil'ssake. Therefore, there are different levels of evil acts.

Since there are different levels of evil actions, then there must be different kinds of qualities associated with each level. A sadistic spree killer who takes pleasure in his victims' pain is vastly different from a brutal dictator who orders the killing of innocent people and justifies it in the name of greater good.

THERE DOES NOT EXIST a list of qualities that are shown by an evildoer, rather there are qualities that are *shared* by evil people. These qualities are varied and many, such as the unequivocal belief that the evildoers are right, egoism, sadism, narcissism, deceitfulness, Machiavellianism—the belief that ends justify the means, lack of empathy, moral disengagement, entitlement, and manipulation, among many others. These psychological qualities are commonplace in human psychology, but they are also morally significant.

THESE QUALITIES CAN BE SEEN in the actions and thoughts of many evildoers from age to age and culture to culture.

THE MEGALOMANIAC Who Knew Best

POL POT, the Communist leader of the Khmer Rouge, Cambodia's Communist Regime, murdered almost 1/4th of his country's population to achieve his vision. Pol Pot wanted to create a classless agrarian society that rejected capitalism, religion, money, and the influence of the West. He wanted to return Cambodia to the glory of the Angkor Empire before it fell under the influence of the corrupt foreigners.

To implement his vision, Pol Pot first marched into the capital Phnom Penh, emptied the cities, abolished money, free markets, schooling, private property, foreign clothing styles, entertainment, public gatherings, and religious practices. Then he arrested and killed anyone who was not "pure"—mostly anyone who supported the previous regime, was educated, or believed in capitalism—as well as ethnic Vietnamese and Cham Muslims.

Thousands of soldiers, politicians and bureaucrats were killed. All the leftover people in the cities, even children, were taken to the countryside to work in labor camps. Pol Pot planned to grow rice and other agricultural products and believed that the large enough production would be used in trade with other countries.

He essentially wanted to take Cambodia back to the Dark Ages.

Unfortunately, in the first year, starvation wreaked havoc on the population, so the harvest was not good. Pol Pot saw it as a failure and loss of control over the regime. He blamed the people within the regime.

So, in retaliation, he started killing anyone who was a dissident (communist or not), anyone who disagreed with any of his opinions, or was recalcitrant. He killed hundreds of thousands of peasants and urban evacuees. Often people who wore glasses were killed. Hundreds of thousands of middle-class people were tortured and executed in death camps. The most notorious of these camps was S-21 jail in Phnom Penh, Tuol Sleng, where more than 15,000 men, women, and children were imprisoned.

. . .

IN THE NAME of his radical utopia, the Pol Pot had turned most of his people into slaves. Husbands were separated from wives, children from parents. People were told whom to marry and how to live, and any who disobeyed were killed. Children informed on their parents; many other children who did not bend to the regime's propaganda were buried alive, tossed into the air and speared on bayonets, or fed to crocodiles.

POL POT SHOWED the qualities of Machiavellianism—the belief that ends justify the means, megalomania, lack of empathy, denial, and moral disengagement, among many others. A supporter who visited him in exile reported, "He said... There were people to whom he felt very close, and he trusted them completely. Then in the end they made a mess of everything." These words show that Pol Pot believed that he was not responsible for anything that happened to his people and was thus unremorseful of his actions.

. . .

He thought that he had fought a holy war and that his people had betrayed him by messing everything up. He, himself, had never meant to kill anyone.

The Leader Who Committed Genocide

"To be frank with you, had we killed all of them, the ten point three million [European Jews], I would be happy and say, 'All right, we managed to destroy an enemy.' " said Eichmann to a former Dutch Nazi when he was in exile in Argentina.

Adolf Eichmann, the Jewish expert of the SS, was the person in charge of carrying out various schemes to remove the Jews from Germany. He ensured that the Jews who lived in Germany, in Poland, and later in the Soviet Union (after Germany invaded it in 1941), along with Jews from every part of Europe under Nazi control, were deported to ghettos and later into camps, such as Auschwitz, to be murdered.

. . .

DIETER WISLICENY SAID that Eichmann told him that he would “"leap laughing into the grave because the feeling that he had five million people on his conscience would be for him a source of extraordinary satisfaction".

IN 1944, Eichmann transported thousands of Jewish people to Auschwitz concentration camp, where more than 70% were killed on arrival. He became responsible for killing over 450,000 Hungarian Jews.

FIVE YEARS after the end of the world war II, Adolf Eichmann escaped from Germany and moved to Argentina by using false documents. Ten years later, a team of Mossad agents captured him and brought him to stand trial for his crimes. Eichmann was subjected to daily interrogations by the police in order to confirm his actions.

AT FIRST EICHMANN lied or was evasive when describing his actions during the Nazi regime, but when documents provided by Nazi hunter Tuviah Friedman came into the hands of the police, Eichmann started to insist that he had been used as a tool in the Nazi hierarchy. He insisted that he was only following orders.

"THERE IS a need to draw a line between the leaders responsible and the people like me forced to serve as mere instruments in the hands of the leaders", Eichmann wrote. "I was not a responsible leader, and as such do not consider myself guilty."

EICHMANN'S INTERROGATOR Inspector Less even said that Eichmann did not realize the extent of his actions and was not the least bit remorseful about them. "It made no difference to me," Eichmann casually declared on one recording, "where the Jews went, as far as I was concerned they could have marched to Madagascar, or gone to Globocnik to be gassed, as far as I was concerned they could have gone to Auschwitz, or to Riga."

CYNICAL, pitiless, deceitful, morally corrupt, Machiavellian—these are all inadequate descriptors for Eichmann, who was a fanatical believer in the right of the Reich to rule. He was not evil because he showed all the common traits found in evil people, rather he was evil because he did serious and excessive harm to Jewish people.

Judgement

Both individuals in the examples above showed qualities that are commonly shared by evil people—deceitfulness, Machiavellianism—the belief that ends justify means, lack of empathy, moral disengagement, entitlement, and manipulation, among many others.

However, it is not these qualities that made these people evil; it was the harm they caused to other human beings that made them evil. They were not classified as evil just because they lacked empathy or were morally corrupt; they were classified as evil because they killed millions of people.

6

THE TEMPTATION OF EVIL.

"The greatest temptations are not those that solicit our consent to obvious sin, but those that offer us great evils masking as the greatest goods."

— Thomas Merton, No Man Is an Island

What Is Temptation?

Temptation is the desire to do something wrong or unwise, something that endangers long-term goals. It is an immediate urge or impulse to do something. It is indicative of lack of self-control, something that allures and excites someone.

From the religious perspective, temptation is the way that leads to sin. It can cause one to disregard religious beliefs and makes wrong decisions likely.

At times, temptation can be harmless, such as the temptation for delicious food, beautiful clothes, or handsome tools. At other times it can lead one to evil actions.

Consequences of Temptation

Would it not be tempting to humiliate the girl that spread slander about you in high school? Would it not it feel really good if you could take what you wanted when you wanted regardless of anyone's opinions? What could you not do with more power?

. . .

Temptation can lead a person to make wrong decisions. It blinds its victim temporarily so that they cannot see the consequences of their actions. Let's go through an example of a girl who was tempted to get her sister's attention and got something worse.

What Was Done

Delilah was a fourteen-year-old girl with black hair, green eyes and a sharp pointed face. She was short, stick-thin. She looked like a pixie who had somehow fallen into a family of giants. She was out-spoken, opinionated, and brash. After all, she thought, what was a beating in comparison to speaking her mind? She had been tongue-lashed by her mother every day of her life because she looked different from all her family. What was a little bluster in the face of that?

The thing was that Delilah was different from everyone in her family. Her siblings, parents, and grandparents were blonde haired and blue eyed. She was the odd one out with her green eyes and black hair. This difference caused no end of tension between her parents.

Her mother despised her for bringing this all on her; she had always been faithful but her husband despised her. Delilah's father never looked at her because he believed she was not his. Her sister was kind to her in private but even she spread snide rumours about Delilah to her friends. She explained to Delilah once that she could not be seen helping her because it would ruin her prospects for marriage. Besides, Mother would only get angry at Christine. Only Delilah's two brothers, who were both a decade older than her, treated her as their own. But even they left for adventure and she was left alone.

Christine, only five years older than Delilah, married the governor's son and moved into his house. Delilah had no one in her family who was kind to her anymore.

One day, Delilah had just come back from the farm. Her feet were muddy, her clothes were crumpled, and there were twigs in her hair. Delilah was just going inside the house when Christine came out. She saw her little sister, sneered, and asked who Delilah had taken a tumble with.

Delilah had not expected such vitriol from her own sister and was thus speechless. Christine taking this as confirmation, told Delilah that the apple didn't fall far from the tree, did it? Then she swept out of the house, leaving Delilah the recipient of her father's ire and her mother's lash. Gossip swept through the household about what she did and no matter how much she justified herself, nobody ever believed her.

Five years passed; Delilah grew up. A woman of nineteen, she drew many stares. She had grown from a stick-thin wraith into a beautiful young lady. But it was not her beauty that attracted stares. Everywhere she went, gossip followed. Rumours of her loose morals, of her illegitimacy, and of her out-spoken nature. So, she hid in the house as much as possible until she had to go out.

. . .

THEN, Delilah made a friend. Delilah's maid was changed when she turned eighteen. Her new maid knew nothing about her history, or if she knew, did not say anything. They began a fast friendship. Delilah talked to her about everything. She had never experienced this freedom before and she took advantage of it while she had it. In those talks, Rose mentioned that she had a little sister who had once turned her hair blue to get her attention.

DELILAH'S CURIOSITY WAS PIQUED.

SHE ASKED FOR CLARIFICATION, and Rose told her the whole tale. How she ingested the potion and how it turned her hair blue. Rose did not tell Delilah about the consequences, and she did not think to ask.

DELILAH WAS TEMPTED. Could she? Could she use the potion to get her sister's attention? Christine never even talked to her anymore. In fact, she never even came to the house anymore. She always seemed sick.

Delilah hesitated. Surely it would not be best to irritate her sister while she was sick? She questioned herself and found that she did not want to do that to her sister at all. But the thought remained in her head for weeks afterwards.

Then the day came when her sister ran into their house, a huge smile on her face. She ran to her mother and told her something that made them both cry. Delilah, as usual, was not invited.

Delilah hesitated and wondered if she should go and eavesdrop. But then, she shrugged to herself. It was market day: the only day she was allowed to go out. She would not get the chance to go out again for a month. She bit her lip and made her decision.

. . .

As she wandered through the markets, a pastry in her hand, she found a hawker who was selling potions. Intrigued, Delilah went closer. The hawker saw her and asked her what she would like. Delilah, remembering the blue hair prank, suggested to the hawker a prank potion. Something that could turn the hair blue. The hawker grinned slyly and handed her a bottle, saying that one drop of it in water would turn hair blue.

Delilah was satisfied. She wanted Christine to pay a little attention to her. If Rose's sister succeeded in doing that, then Delilah would too. After coming back from the market, she sneaked into her mother's herb room—where her mother prepared a draught for Christine every day. Sneaking was surprisingly easy because her mother was not at home.

She hesitated as she started to lift the lid of the draught. She wondered if she should stop. She hesitated for a while, until her excitement got the better of her. She *wanted* her sister to give her some attention. The urge inside her was almost overwhelming. She mixed the potion into the draught and slipped out.

In her excitement, she had not thought about what her sister would do. She did not think about the consequences of her action.

The prank was meant to be harmless.

What Delilah did not know was that Christine was finally with child after trying for five years. She was overjoyed and scared that she would lose the baby. And lose it she did. When Christine drank that sleep potion, she could not sleep, she felt sick. In the early hours of the morning, even with her mother trying her best to save him or her, her child slipped from her belly.

Delilah woke up that day expecting to be confronted by Christine's blue hair, instead she met a pale and grey woman who couldn't stop sobbing as she lay on the bed, half her body paralyzed.

. . .

DELILAH ONLY WANTED her sister to realise how hard everything had been for her. She only wanted to make Christine pay attention to her. Since childhood she had been neglected by both her father and her mother. The only people who paid any attention to her were her brothers, who left when she was twelve. Delilah had turned to her sister for understanding, but Christine knew that consorting with her ruined sister would destroy her prospects for marriage, so she decided to treat Delilah just like everybody else.

DELILAH WAS UNDERSTANDABLY HEARTBROKEN to find out that her sister was acting towards her in this way. Her kind words had vanished, and in their place was vitriol so thick that it brought tears to Delilah's eyes.

DELILAH BELIEVED that it was not her fault that she had been born with a different hair and eye color. She thought she had her mother's crooked nose, and her father's high cheekbones. She saw herself in her siblings and in the paintings of her great-grand-mother. But, nobody saw any of that. They only saw a mistake.

After Christine was married, Delilah had held out hope that her sister would reach out a hand, but she never did. Delilah had grown up by then. She had been beaten by her mother and shunned by her father every day.

Delilah wanted her sister's attention. She was desperate to get it. So, she pulled a prank, just like she had heard from Ruby. She expected it to be harmless, it was not.

Failed Justification

Defenders of Delilah's actions would say that she was a young woman with no experience at all about anything. She had been sheltered all her life. She had been kept indoors by her mother who took out her anger on Delilah. She had been condemned to an existence for a sin she had no part in. Even though she had been through horrible things, Delilah lacked understanding of many things.

THEY WOULD SAY that her actions were accidental. That she was wrong to do what she did. They would argue that Delilah killed her sister's child and paralyzed her in ignorance.

Condemnation

IGNORANCE DOES NOT REMOVE responsibility from the shoulders of the evildoer. Evil actions cause serious harm to their victim. Delilah, however horrified she may have been, caused serious harm to her sister. She unknowingly caused her to lose a child and to become paralyzed. She showed vincible ignorance—she did something wrong when she ought to have known better.

THEREFORE, despite her ignorance, Delilah committed an act of great evil, and is responsible for it.

Conclusion

In the end, evil is tempting because it can provide answers to things or ease of access to things that you would not get by ascribing to moral agents.

7

MORALITY AND EVIL.

"God made all things good; man meddles with them and they become evil."

—Jean-Jacques Rousseau

WHAT ARE MORALS? HOW IS MORALITY characterized? What do we think of as an admirable moral character? How does one become virtuous? Are we taught by someone to be virtuous? Or, do we become virtuous naturally?

. . .

In this chapter we will explore what morality is, why it varies from individual to individual or culture to culture, and why the concept of morality is disputed. We will also discuss the relationship between the absence of morality and evil and if some evil actions are morally excusable.

What Is Morality?

Morality refers to the most important code of conduct put forward by and accepted by an individual, a group, or even a society. This code of conduct applies to everyone who can understand it and can govern their behavior by it. It contains prohibitions on harming others and can vary from individual to individual or even culture to culture. Stephen Toulmin describes morality as a code that is related to human welfare. He said that it makes communities avoid actions that lead to the suffering of their people. Baier claimed morality was "the good of everyone alike", while Gert thought that it was the lessening of evil or harm.

. . .

Utilitarian scholars, such as Mill, note that morality produces the greatest possible good while lessening harm by prohibiting murder, causing pain, deceiving, and breaking promises. For them every moral precept, such as helping the needy, encourages good and discourages evil. John Stuart Mill even defined morality as, "the rules and precepts for human conduct, by the observance of which a happy existence might be, to the greatest extent possible, secured."

Moral realists, on the other hand, while believing that morality prohibits one from killing, causing pain, deceiving, and breaking promises, also believe that while morality requires charitable actions, the failure to act charitably on every possible occasion does not render one immoral.

For both Immanuel Kant and John Stuart Mill, morality is separated into duties of perfect obligation and duties of imperfect obligation. Perfect obligation to morality regards not harming, such as prohibiting causing pain or deceiving, as its duty, while imperfect obligation requires helping, such as helping the needy, as its duty. Bernard Gert, in contrast, writes that morality does encourage charitable actions, such as giving alms to the poor, but does not require it. Gert essentially says that it is morally good to be charitable, but it is not immoral to not be charitable.

"NATURAL LAW" theories as put forward by Aquinas, claim that any rational person in a society, even one with a defective morality, is capable of knowing what kind of actions are prohibited, discouraged, encouraged, allowed, and required by morality. Theological theories of natural law claim that humans have the knowledge about what is right or wrong because God planted this knowledge within our reason. Secular theories of natural law, such as the one presented by Hobbes, claim that natural reason is sufficient for allowing rational persons to know what morality prohibits and allows.

JUST AS A RELIGIOUS or a legal code can have a vast content, as long as they are capable of guiding behavior, morality accounts place very few limits on the content of a moral code. However, some non-religiously influenced scholars such as Thomas Hobbes limit morality to behavior that, either indirectly or directly, affects others.

THERE IS OFTEN confusion around the concept of morality because most of the time morality is not sufficiently distinguished from religion. Morality is only a guide to conduct, whereas religion is more than that. Religions may prohibit or require more than is called for by moral guides, they may even recommend some behavior that is prohibited by morality. Some religious practices and precepts can also be criticized on moral grounds, such as the practice of discrimination on the basis of gender, race, or sexual orientation. Even when morality is not put forward by formal religion, it often requires some religious explanation or justification.

BUT, if morality is separated from religion, the content of moral rules is limited to behavior that directly or indirectly causes or risks harm to others. Some behavior that seems to affect an individual, e.g., taking drugs, may have a significant indirect harmful effect on others by supporting the illegal and harmful activity of those who benefit from the sale of those drugs.

MORALITY IS a concept that is much disagreed upon in the scholarly community. Morals are culture-based. A man in one culture can grow up believing that wearing short sleeves is forbidden because his morals state that it is, while another in some other culture can think that incest is permissible when the few accepted tenants of moral laws explicitly forbid it.

MORALS ARE ALSO TIME-DEPENDENT. They change over time. A few decades ago, certain behaviors such as entering into same-sex relationships, engaging in pre-martial sexual relationships were forbidden and found to be morally unacceptable by the majority of the population, to the extent that people were killed for breaking these morals. Nowadays, these behaviors are considered morally acceptable by a vast majority of the population.

. . .

THESE EXAMPLES SHOW the mutable nature of morality, that it can change and adjust according to time and culture. They also show that the moral code followed in one part of the world may not be followed in another part of the world.

SO, in simple words, morality is a code of conduct (beliefs and values) about what is right and what is wrong or acceptable and unacceptable. There exist only a few moral concepts that are accepted by everyone, such as murder, rape, breaking of promises, and incest, as well as the moral duty to treat others as you would like to be treated. But most of the time this code is not concrete, rather it is personal to each and every individual or society.

EVIL: Connection with Morality

EVIL IS excessive serious harm done to human beings by human beings, such as murder, serial killing, and rape, among many others, that is inexcusable. It cannot be explained away as self-defense, unexpected consequence, or ignorance. Morality is the complete opposite. It is the code of conduct that is used by individuals and the society as a whole to *prevent* evil actions from happening. Morals are beliefs and values that people implement in order to make sure that their actions do not disturb or harm other individuals or society as a whole.

If morality is used to seek happiness or lessening of harm then evil does the opposite. Evil actions harm human beings irrevocably, while the morality limits the *possibility* of harm done to people. Evil actions go beyond breaking moral rules; they show contempt for and flaunt fundamental moral prohibitions. Moral rules, in contrast, discourage evil and try to ensure that it never takes place through harsh unopposable condemnation.

Therefore, if evil harms others and morality tries to prevent harm to others then evil is the absence of morality. Morality ceases to exist when actions that harm people take place.

Let's take the example of Maximillian Robespierre, the man who started the Reign of Terror in France during the French Revolution. Robespierre thought he knew best, that he was the only one pure enough to see the right path for his corrupted nation, so when he gained his office he tried to impose his views on others. At first, many were delighted because he had given them leave to finally unleash their worst urges. Royal families were guillotined, princesses were torn apart and disemboweled, women were raped and buried alive, young children were killed and buried alive, in short, unspeakable atrocities took place in that time, all in the name of purifying the nation.

When certain people, especially Robespierre's supporters started to decry the atrocities being committed, they were guillotined. Anyone who dared speak against Robespierre and his terrible actions was killed without mercy. Robespierre even said, "There are only two parties in France: the people and its enemies.

We must exterminate those miserable villains who are eternally conspiring against the rights of man… We must exterminate all our enemies."

He technically said that anyone who opposed him and his just regime was an enemy of France, that these "enemies" didn't want him to build a better nation. So, he allowed the mob in Paris and the dissatisfied people in other cities to commit atrocities, all because he thought he knew best.

Are Robespierre's actions excused because he thought he was doing the right thing? He was trying to make his nation better, was he not ? He wanted to get France out from the tyranny of the Royal family, did he not ? Are his actions excusable?

They most certainly are not. In fact, Robespierre egged on his supporters (the mob in Paris) to do their worst. They certainly did not disappoint. Robespierre believed that he knew what was best for the people of France. He thought that only he could bring France to a better place and he left no stone unturned in order to reach his goal. He allowed the murder of innocents, he allowed lynching, disemboweling, shooting down women and children, burying people alive, and tearing people limb from limb. He allowed atrocities to occur that he had the power to stop.

So, are his actions excusable? No, they most certainly are not. Robespierre was a lawyer and an intelligent peer of the realm. He knew how to separate facts from opinions. He knew the basics of morality and what is right and what is wrong. He knew what was unacceptable and acceptable. He argued over laws and he broke all of them.

Robespierre's actions were inexcusable under moral laws because he knew that he was deliberately harming people and chose to ignore that fact in order to achieve his goal. In fact, at times he even told his supporters to do more in their fight for a new France.

. . .

But, what about evil actions that are actually *excusable* under moral laws? Can murder be excusable under moral law?

Let's take the example of a man named Darius, a man of military bearing who had just come back home from his office. Darius was sitting with his wife and daughter, eating dinner, when the door to his home splintered as if it had been punched by a giant.

Following the splinters of the door were a few men, armed and aggressive, who walked into the house as if they owned it. Darius, who had survived some years through the army, always kept a gun at hand. When he heard the door splinter, Darius grabbed his gun from a cabinet and ordered his wife and daughter to run into his study and lock themselves in. He would *not* let any harm come to them.

He counted the footsteps of the men and knew that there were more men than he could safely dispatch without killing. He knew he had no choice. He crouched behind the island in his kitchen and watched them as they entered the kitchen, all clad in bulletproof vests, their guns held steady, their steps careful and slow. He heard someone, their commander probably, asking them to spread around the house.

He heard the sound of gunfire and a loud shrilling scream rang out through the house. His daughter's scream.

FEAR GRIPPED HIM. He could not go help his family. Another scream rang out. Then two shots rang out. A man screamed and fell silent.

DARIUS HAD to go to them.

DARIUS COUNTED TO TEN, stood up with blinding speed, and emptied three bullets into the three men. Each caught them in their nose and eyebrow area—in their T-Zone. They fell to the floor, dead on impact. It was the most effective way to disable the threat.

. . .

He ran out into the main hall and hid behind a couch.

Hearing the gunshots, two other men ran into the kitchen and emptied a magazine into the kitchen table, island, and kitchen appliances. They stepped into the main hall; their steps cautious. When they neared him, Darius jumped out, shot one soldier dead and threw him at his partner. Darius got off a shot before he fell down. Ice slid through his side. Then came the pain. He staggered.

The man threw his partner off, but before he could stand up, Darius shot him dead. He ran towards his study and found a man crouched by his partner's mangled body. He turned when he heard Darius' footsteps. Darius didn't let him aim. He emptied his clip into the man and walked deeper into the house to make sure that there was nobody else in the house, aware that his daughter might be dying at that moment.

Could Darius have done anything else? Could he have run? Was there no other option left to him?

He clearly could not have done anything else. His daughter and wife were there in the house with him. He had to protect them at all costs. He knew that there was no other way for his wife and child to survive if he did not kill these men.

Can Darius be excused for his actions? Did he not commit an evil action when he killed those men? Did he not perform excessive harm to those men? Do his good intentions repeal the fact that he committed an evil action?

Darius has committed an evil action. He has brought about harm to seven other men. He killed them to protect his wife and children, but he still *murdered* them. Murder is regarded as an inexcusable evil act because it does significant harm to other human beings. However, in this instance, Darius used force to defend himself and his wife and daughter.

There was no other reason why he killed those men.

In Darius' case, he was not the aggressor, the men who attacked him were. Darius had no evil intent, while his attackers did. They violated the boundary of his home and used force in order to try and kill him and his family. Darius did not murder them out of ill will, malevolence, rage, or hatred. Rather he had to neutralize them because he had to ensure the survival of his family.

This justification holds because according to the law Darius was right to defend himself and his family when they were threatened. The *violent aggressors* wanted to harm Darius and his family. They had criminal intent. They also succeeded when they shot Darius's daughter. Darius knew that in order to save his family, he had to live, and to live, *he had to* nullify the threat. He took no pleasure in the act. Darius did not care about himself; he was solely focused on the survival of his family.

. . .

THEREFORE, it is clear that there are times when murder or any other evil action can be morally excusable if it can be proven that the person who has committed an evil action had no evil intent in the first place.

8

EVIL ACTIONS: WHO WILL TAKE RESPONSIBILITY?

"This is the excellent foppery of the world, that, when we are sick in fortune . . . we make guilty of our disasters the sun, the moon, the stars; as if we were villains by necessity, fools by compulsion, knaves, thieves, and treachers by spherical predominance, drunkards, liars, and adulterers by an enforced obedience to planetary influence; and all that we are evil in, by a divine thrusting on: an admirable evasion of whoremaster man."

—William Shakespeare, King Lear

Many people exempt evildoers from responsibility either due to religious views, such as the view that all human beings are sinners because of the fall, or because they think that all human beings are basically good and only commit evil because political arrangements corrupt us—as stated in the Enlightenment view. These views are used to excuse evildoers from being responsible for their actions because the apologists think that anyone could become evil if exposed to the same causes. They confess that they might also have become evildoers if they had been in the evildoers' place and gain sympathy for the evildoers, all at the expense of the victim.

They say that the intention of the evildoer matters. If they did the work deliberately, that is one thing, but if they did not intend their actions, then it is quite another. So, if evildoers are motivated by sincere but false beliefs, then the question arises whether it is justified to hold them responsible. If their actions were unintentional, are they excused from the responsibility of their actions?

. . .

It is a well-regarded opinion in all circles of debate that an evildoer must be held responsible for their evil actions because these actions have caused serious harm to fellow human beings. To call someone evil is to acknowledge that they are a moral agent. Moral agents can only perform evil actions when they are held morally responsible for them. Their actions also have to be inexcusable, done voluntarily, bear ill will to their victim, and be inexcusable.

Most of the times these tenants are met when holding mass murderers, serial killers, and other kinds of evildoers responsible for their actions. However, these tenants become hard to meet in a few kinds of cases where the evildoer is either insane or suffers an impairment, whether self-produced or not.

Responsibility for Evil

Let's take the example of Robespierre, the man who waged war against the moderates in the

French Revolution, who he claimed were the enemies of humanity and were to be eradicated from the face of the earth. He further claimed that he was protecting moral ideals against these attackers. Robespierre had people buried alive, torn to pieces, slowly drowned, lynched, humiliated, and parts of their still warm bodies devoured by the Paris mob. He incited his underlings to throw babies into crematoriums, bury children alive, and suffocate a pregnant woman by hanging her from the rafters while plunging a knife into her a dozen times.

Did Robespierre not cause excessive harm to the people of France when he unleashed the Terror on them? Should he not be held responsible for his actions?

Let's consider the case of the crusaders before making a judgment. In 1209, the Albigensian Crusade started because the Pope declared war on Cathars, who he said were trying to subvert Christianity. He claimed that knights had to defend the honor and moral ideals of their religion against these attackers. The knights traveled to the Cathars and waged war on them, believing that they had moral justification. They killed children, threw people in wells, tore out their eyes, cut off their ears, and burned them alive. They also killed anyone who ever helped the Cathars, and even killed their entire families. They spared no one in their crusade against the Cathars.

Both Robespierre and the crusaders claimed that they were doing good for humanity, when in fact what they did was far in excess of what was covered by their justification of moral ideals. Their false beliefs do not even begin to justify the malevolent savagery and inhuman cruelty shown in their actions. Even if we accept that it was necessary to kill their opponents, it was unnecessary to torture them. They could have also imprisoned them or exiled them. There were many ways to deal with those people, rampant torture and malevolent savagery were not two of them.

According to John Kekes, "Seeing what is wrong with [evildoers], however, helps to explain that evil actions cause excessive and malevolent harm because of the evildoers' passions. These passions are aroused because evildoers see their victims as threatening the ideal that makes, or would make, their lives meaningful and is, or would be, the source of their identity and psychological security. Their excesses and malevolence are due to the passions with which they are defending what is most important in their lives. Evildoers, of course, are rarely aware that this is what motivates them, and their victims are rarely attacking them. Layers and layers of falsification lie between how the evildoers see the facts and the facts themselves."

BUT WHAT IF the evildoers became clear-sighted enough to realize that their pursuit of their passions might lead them to commit evil actions? If the evildoers are passionate enough for their cause that they are willing to sacrifice thousands of innocent people, then it is important to realize that they won't stop committing evil actions when they realize what they are doing. The only difference their clear-sightedness (which is very rare) will possibly make is that now they will do evil with full understanding, rather than through self-deception.

. . .

It is also important to realize that an action is not labeled as evil because it is caused by ignorance of morality or knowledge, rather it also labeled as evil because of the evildoers' motives. If the above-mentioned clarity gives the evildoer knowledge of their actions, their motives may still not change.

Most evildoers like to pay lip-service to morality in order to convince themselves that the harm they are causing is not inspired by malevolence but rather by justifiable moral ideals. They do not want to be judged by their peers, so they falsify facts in order to be exempt from responsibility. They do not wish to believe that they abused their ideals, faith, ideology and honor.

Excusing evildoers from responsibility for their actions because their false beliefs made their evil actions unintentional is wrong because these evildoers would still be held responsible for their actions even if their false beliefs were true. Their moral explanations do not justify their excesses and savagery because morality protects human well-beings while they did the opposite. They would also still have the motivation to commit these evil actions whether due to their faith, ambition, honor, moral ideals, or ideology even if they became clear-sighted.

Intention

INTENTION AND RESPONSIBILITY are intimately connected. Usually, people are held responsible for their intentional actions, the actions they choose to do, the actions whose moral significance they understand. This means that responsibility is directly linked to intention. But, what about unintentional actions? Should people be held responsible for them too?

ONE MAIN REASON for holding people responsible for their actions is that they have caused significant harm to their fellow human beings. If they have done evil, this attitude is appropriate. But would it still be appropriate if the evildoer was insane or incapacitated in some way? If they could not form intentions because they could not understand the weight of their choices, then they may not be held responsible for their actions. But if the evildoer was incapacitated by their choice, for example they were knowingly ignorant, then they could also be held responsible for their actions and their impairment both.

The evil action of an insane or incapacitated person is very different from one who is drunk for example. Both might inflict harm unintentionally, but the drunk has the ability to reason and understand his choices while the insane or impaired one does not. Therefore, it might—or might not—be appropriate to hold someone responsible for their intentional evil actions, depending on why their evil actions were not intentional.

Consider two people with identical intentions to perform an evil action, let's say to murder an innocent person. One succeeds, but the other doesn't because the victim escapes or is not caught in the first place. If responsibility depended on intention, then both the successful and would-be murderers would carry the same responsibility. But in reality, they do not have the same responsibility because only one murderer did any harm to their victim. We can decry the intention of the would be-murderer, but only because we are aware that their intention would have led to an evil action.

This shows that responsibility depends on evil actions, not intention. If one person has harmed another person substantially, then they should technically carry the responsibility of their actions. This means that intentions are used to assign responsibility to the evildoer, but only because they precipitate the evil action.

Let's take the example of a slave owner in a society where slavery has been an accepted practice since time immemorial. Slaves are regarded as subhuman and little better than animals. Therefore, they are not treated as humans should be treated. This particular slave owner treats his slaves no better or worse than other people. He buys and sells them, works them hard, gifts them to his servants, and whips them when they are unruly. He is only doing what other people around him do. He does not need to justify the practice to himself because it would be like trying to justify having trees, or keeping servants in his house. He does have a choice in being a slave owner, but he does not understand the significance of the choice he made when he began thinking about his slaves as subhuman. Therefore, he is not an intentional slave owner. He is only a slave owner because everyone around him is.

But are his actions not evil? Even if he did not intend to enslave people, he is still doing it. Is he exempt from the responsibility of his actions? No, he is not. Even if he did not intend to harm other human beings, he is still doing it. This means that he is breaking the laws of morality, as morality is concerned with human well-being, and is thus classified as evil. Therefore, he should be held accountable for his actions, even if he did them unintentionally.

Thus sometimes—not all the time—it may be appropriate to hold people responsible for their unintentionally evil actions because if it was not appropriate to hold people responsible for their unintentional actions, then it would be inappropriate to hold the evildoers responsible for their evil actions since their false beliefs made it hard for them to understand the overarching significance of their actions.

In simple words, all evildoers work from a pit of false belief, which is unintentional. If they were excused of responsibility for their unintentional beliefs, they would essentially be excused for their intentional evil actions. This would make it hard to condemn these evildoers because their unintentional beliefs bade them take unintentional actions.

Therefore, it is always appropriate to hold evildoers who have committed intentional evil actions responsible for them. But, it is not always appropriate to hold evildoers who have committed unintentional evil actions responsible for them unless they the evildoers are responsible for the impairment that makes them unable to understand the significance of their actions.

. . .

Conclusion

THE EVIL ACTIONS, such as murder, torture, and mutilation, of the crusaders and Maximilian Robespierre caused serious harm to their victims that prevented them from living their lives. They could have achieved their goals by jailing or exiling their victims. There was no need to burn them alive, mutilate them, cannibalize them, or hand them to a mob to be tortured. These incidents show that these evildoers were not indifferent to the suffering of their victims, rather they were bent on causing as much suffering to them as they could. These actions were nottaken only once; they were actions that were habitual, where deliberate harm was caused to innocent victims again and again.

THE SERIOUSNESS of the harm caused by these evildoers is evident, as is the evidence for it. No excuse justifies or absolves these evildoers from responsibility for their actions, and neither does it lower the significance of the harm caused by the evildoers.

. . .

THEREFORE, it is clear that evildoers should be held responsible for their intentional evil actions and, at times, even their unintentionally evil actions, provided the evildoers are responsible for the impairment that causes them to overlook the significance of their actions themselves.

THE PATH TO THE DARKSIDE: PUSH AND PULL FACTORS.

WHY DO WE TURN TO EVIL? WHAT FACTORS PROMPT US TO COMMIT EVIL?

In this section, we will discuss the factors that draw us or push us towards evil. We will discuss the role played by social disparity, prejudice, tunnel-vision, ignorance, volatile emotions, will, and expectations in making us turn to the dark side.

1

XENOPHOBIA: US VS. THEM MENTALITY.

"The pleasure in complete domination over another person (or other animate creature) is the very essence of the sadistic drive. Another way of formulating the same thought is to say that the aim of sadism is to transform man into a thing, something animate into something inanimate, since by complete and absolute control the living loses one essential quality of life - freedom."

—Erich Fromm

At its core, xenophobia is prejudice. Prejudice is actively disliking, being hostile, or bearing ill will towards other people or things. Prejudice stems from intolerant, preconceived and unproven or baseless opinions. A prejudice can be held against anything or anyone. People can be biased towards short clothes, such as short skirts or shorts, or towards skin color.

Xenophobia, on the other hand, is active dislike or fear shown by *human beings* towards other *human beings*. It is the fear or hatred of strangers or anyone who is different from us—anyone who is "other". Xenophobia stems from the ancient Greek words, xénos, meaning stranger or guest, and phóbos meaning fear or panic. This means that xenophobia stems from fear.

Xenophobia can manifest itself in several different ways, such as avoidance of certain people and areas, refusing to come into contact with people because they are different, i.e., have a different skin color, society, religion, dress code, etc., and feeling uncomfortable with anyone "other".

Xenophobic people usually believe that their culture, ethnicity, nation, and race, among other factors, is superior and above everyone else. They want to keep any "outsider" out of their society, and can go to great lengths to do this, even massive acts of violence and destruction against other groups of people.

Since Xenophobia stems from fear and hatred, qualities which rely on subjective experiences that are particular to every individual, it calls for objectification and naming of these "others". Xenophobic people, at first, label the feared object or person and denigrate it. Later the fear of the "other" becomes integrated into social values, which in turn modulate the intensity of the fear and can change it into hatred of these "others".

Erich Fromm, in his study of prejudice, identified that when the social character of people belonging to the same group changes—they feel more dominating, freer, powerful, secure in the knowledge that there is someone who is beneath them—then group narcissism occurs. They feel superior to the people who oppose them.

He further said that group narcissism is fostered in societies which are particularly interested in maintaining economic differences among people. Pearson et al. confirmed this and concluded that those who seek to maintain economic differences among people in a society have a greater likelihood of being prejudiced than those who believe in an equal distribution of resources.

Xenophobia: How It Relates to Evil

Xenophobia comes in two forms: cultural and stranger xenophobia. Cultural xenophobia occurs when anything such as language, history, and traditions of a group is rejected by another group. Stranger xenophobia occurs when an individual who is "other"—who does not belong to a community or nation in the eyes of the xenophobic person—is rejected. This rejection can lead to hostility and discrimination, persecution, destruction, hate crimes, and in the worst times, to war and genocide.

THIS ATTITUDE CAN MAKE it difficult for the group being discriminated against to live within a society because employment opportunities, housing, aid, and the good opinion of their colleagues dries up. This kind of hatred can be seen leveled throughout history against a great number of people. The Cathars were killed to a man by the Crusaders in the 13th century. The crusaders cut off their noses and ears, raped their women, threw them into wells, dismembered them, and burned them alive because they believed they were superior to the Cathars.

SIMILARLY, during the Middle Ages, when the Black Plague was wreaking havoc across Europe, Jews were burned alive and killed indiscriminately because it was believed that they were the cause of this plague.

. . .

Xenophobia carries a great potential to cause serious harm to others. It can result in wars, destruction, and genocide of people who have done nothing wrong—who are innocent. It can force the prejudiced party to commit atrocities, such as mass murder, rape, disemboweling, skinning, and burning or burying alive—in their zeal for eliminating the offending party.

If evil is serious harm done by human beings to other human beings, then xenophobia can lead to a human being committing great evil.

Xenophobia in History: Genocide

Xenophobia has been shown by countless people and societies towards other societies and people throughout human history. The ancient Romans and Greeks used their belief in their superiority to justify their enslavement of their own and other people. They believed that they had the God-given right to rule over others. Aristotle even said, "For that some should rule and others be ruled is not only necessary, but expedient; from the hour of their birth, some are marked out for subjection, others for rule…"

Xenophobia has led to countless acts of violence, discrimination, and genocide in the world, such as the Holocaust, the Bosnian genocide, the Rwandan genocide, the Armenian genocide, and the Cambodian genocide, among others. The Cambodian genocide, done under the rule of the Khmer Rouge, killed around 2 million people—25% of the Cambodian population at that time. However, of all of these, the Holocaust was the bloodiest genocide in recent history: it killed more than 6 million people.

Hitler and Genocide.

It is uncertain where Hitler's hatred for Jews stems from, but it is assured that it began when he was younger. Hitler's hatred nurtured his prejudice, so xenophobia played a huge role in Hitler's decision to murder the Jews. Jewish people had been victims of discrimination and had been persecuted in Europe since the Middle Ages. They were forced to convert because their religion was perceived as an aberration by the Christians. Some were even burned alive when the Black Plague killed thousands because it was thought they were poisoning wells.

However, in Hitler's time, religion didn't play such a huge role in society, racial theories did. Hitler, inspired by Count Gobineau's racial theory, argued that there was a hierarchy of races based on skin color with the "Aryans"—blue-eyed, blonde haired, and pale skinned people—were at the top, while Gypsies and Blacks were at the bottom. These Aryan people consisted of people from Germany, England, the Netherlands, and Scandinavia.

Jewish people were regarded as subhuman; Hitler even classified them as such. Nazi ideology stated the Jews were clever and had their own plan for world domination. Nazis thought that this plan was extremely dangerous, so it had to be opposed by all Aryans.

Nazis, according to Richard Evans, believed that, "the strong and the racially pure had to be encouraged to have more children, the weak and the racially impure had to be neutralized by one means or another."

In late 1920, Hitler started saying in his speeches and writings that Jews were a "parasite on the body of the people". He considered them a bacterium or a virus that was destroying the nation. He continuously stated that Jewish people were a force of disintegration in Germany, and implied heavily that they may have been the cause of the loss of World War I. This comparison was something like a lifeline to the angered and hopeless people of Germany after the end of World War I, so they seized it with both hands. The sentiment spread through the people of Germany like wildfire, all helped by the charismatic nature of the orator—Hitler—himself.

These radical ideas paved the road for the Final Solution, the purpose of which was to destroy these disease-ridden cells from the body of Germany for all eternity. This was the road through which Hitler, the man who made himself out to be the "Doctor of the German people", the leader who "profoundly recognizes the distress of his people", and then "seriously tries to cure it", committed genocide. Hitler's profound hatred for the Jewish people—his xenophobia towards them—prompted him to take the lives of over 6 million Jewish people who had done nothing to him—who were innocent.

Conclusion

In the end, xenophobia holds the potential to lure people to evil. It can make them cause serious harm to their fellow human beings though actions such as discrimination, persecution, violence, hate crimes, murders, and finally genocide. The Holocaust is just one example of the many genocides committed over history by people under xenophobic tendencies; however, it was the worst.

2

EXPECTATIONS AND EVIL.

"Most people are not even aware of their need to conform. They live under the illusion that they follow their own ideas and inclinations, that they are individualists, that they have arrived at their opinions as the result of their own thinking—and that it just happens that their ideas are the same as those of the majority."

— Erich Fromm, The Art of Loving

What are Expectations?

The word expectation comes from the Latin word "expectationem", meaning " awaiting". An expectation is the belief that something should happen or is going to happen a certain way in the future. They are the beliefs that we use to create hope or anticipation in life. They are overarching beliefs that span our all parts of our lives—our families, our jobs, and our future. They help us envision a future.

Expectations are unique to every individual. They develop through a combination of an individuals' experiences and knowledge. Expectations can be external and internal. Internal expectations are set by an individual for themselves; they are personal expectations of what you expect from yourself in the future. External expectations are what other's expect from you. They are the beliefs of things that others expect you to do.

An example of an internal expectation would be an individual expecting that they'll become a lawyer in the future while they're studying law at law school. They might or might not become one in the future, but they hold the expectation that they might become one in the future. An example of an external expectation, on the other hand, can be a mother expecting her child to grow up pious and modest. She doesn't know what he will turn out to be, but she hopes and expects that he will do good.

But what happens when expectations aren't met or fulfilled? What happens if the baby you raised from birth, who you expected to treat you kindly, turns you out of his house? What if the dream you had from youth, your expectations that you would become a lawyer never came to fruition due to a bad decision?

Role of Expectations in Our Lives

Positive Impacts of Expectations

Expectations help us overcome our fear of taking action, they can fuel hope for something, and they can help a person become better. Consider the case of a young woman who had grown up dreaming she would become a geologist and an astrophysicist. She wanted to be both at once. She loved physics, outer space, and rocks. Everything around her seemed like a marvel. Everything had so many secrets. The girl's parents supported her in everything. They hadn't had enough chances in life. They were determined to give them to their daughter.

The first time she failed in physics, she found that achieving her dream was going to be a bit harder than she thought. She studied day and night until she understood everything. She applied the concepts she had learned to everyday life and learned more than she had thought. Her mother and father disapproved. They thought she was destroying herself in the pursuit of a goal they were not even sure would be good for her. But their daughter was determined.

IT TOOK a few years but she finally succeeded. She became what she had always wanted to be. She had fulfilled her expectations through all her hard work. She loved what she did for a living, and even if they did not approve of her grueling journey, her parents always been beside her.

For the girl, her own expectations led her to do something extraordinary. They helped her pave a path in life that even her parents weren't too sure of. She achieved her dream of doing what she loved. Her expectations gave her hope and gave her the strength to work harder than ever. They helped her reach her goal.

Negative Impacts of Expectations

If expectations can imbue a person with hope and help them overcome obstacles that seem impossible, they can also have the opposite effect. Some expectations can harm a person irrevocably. Others can damage them beyond repair.

Let's consider the case of a man who had been born into an illustrious banking family. He was the only son his mother ever birthed. When he was born he was the most perfect child, calm and sure, respectful and stoic, and intelligent and curious. His mother had huge expectations for him. His father expected that he would one day spearhead the family business.

UNFORTUNATELY, when that child grew up, he had no aptitude for mathematics. He was brilliant at talking to people and make them at ease, but he had no skill for banking. He could not understand accounts, but he understood chemistry. He could not balance any accounting statement to save his life, but he could charm the silver off a woman's throat. Suffice it to say, his family was disappointed: his mother because her husband expected her to produce a better child, his father because he had expected his son to grow up to be an intelligent banker, and his own self because he had not met their expectations.

HE FOUND that he loved chemicals, combinations, and the smell of burned eyebrows. He wanted to be a chemist; his parents wanted him to be a banker. The boy tried his hardest to fit it in; however, he never did. The conflicting expectations of his parents and himself had led him on a path that was hard to come back from. He became a banker by day, running the business and satisfying the clients. But at night, he sought solace in drinking and women. But after a decade of being debauchery, he went to a bar and never came back.

In this case, the expectations of the boy and his parents conflicted so much that they drove their son to drink. Most of the fault lies with the parents. When they realized that their son was never going to be what they wanted, they could have accepted him as he was. However, they did not, and instead pushed him into becoming what he was not. This damaged the boy immensely. This damage led him on a path that eventually destroyed him and his family in the end.

The purpose of these examples was to show how expectations can do both considerable harm and considerable good. They can help an individual reach great heights, but they can also make them fall from great heights.

. . .

Since it has been established that expectation can harm to a human being, the question becomes: what is the extent of the harm they can do? Can they actually make a person commit evil actions? Or, can they limit them from committing an evil action?

Consider the Khmer Rouge and its rule in Cambodia during the 1970s. Pol Pot, when he came to power in the Cambodia due to the Khmer Rouge, implemented his idea of creating an agrarian regime with extreme prejudice. He banned free markets, religion, cultural practices, and education, among other things. He emptied out cities and took out everyone to work in forced labor camps in the countryside. To make sure there were no outbreaks of rebellion, he killed all of the educated people—lawyers, doctors, and intellectuals who could have opposed him.

All these massacres took a toll. When the harvest in the first year came short of the expected amount, Pol Pot—the leader of the Khmer Rouge—was enraged. He thought that the people were not working properly. In his rage, he had anyone who was under suspicion of not working properly killed. Farmers, newly arrived city-dwellers, middle-class people, and even anyone who wore glasses was killed. Anyone else who disagreed with him was either killed or sent to prison. Thousands of men, women, and children were tortured and murdered in the capital city because it was believed they were causing insurrection within the country.

Pol Pot's expectation was to create an agrarian society that shunned the evils of capitalism. He killed thousands of innocent men and women to achieve it. He went as far as to cause thousands of innocent deaths just because of a quota he had set and had not been met. He did not care for the lives of his people, rather he only cared for his vision, his belief of what the future should hold, and he pursued it relentlessly, even committing evil acts in the process.

. . .

However, let's take another example. King Leopold II of Belgium in the late 1800s decided to become a rich man. He loaned his hand in the Congo to rubber companies and expected them to do what they willed in order to obtain the necessary gold. The rubber companies did get him the gold, but they took blood in the process. In order to meet quotas, thousands of men and women of the Congo were forced in labor and became abject slaves.

When the quotas became outrageous, the soldiers who were imposing the law took the right hands of each worker as a payment. Soon enough, as the quotas rose, and so did the piles of hands. At time came when villages cut off the hands of their own people in order to meet quotas. The villages that rebelled were pillaged and their people murdered. Piles of hands were seen in baskets. Children, women, or men—no one was spared.

The King had lent his lands to the rubber companies to gain revenue, not lose it. So, the rubber companies enforced any and every rule in order to make that revenue. They killed and maimed people to fulfill the King's expectations. King Leopold in his desire for wealth had caused the deaths of thousands of innocent people. In the pursuit of the fulfilment of his expectations, he had committed great evil.

JUST LIKE POL POT and King Leopold II, Hitler, the Crusaders, and Robespierre Maximillian committed many evil actions in the name of achieving their expectations. Hitler wanted a pure Germany that was free of the Jewish "parasites" so he exterminated them. The Crusaders wanted the deaths of the "heretic" Cathars so they massacred them through any way possible. Robespierre wanted to establish a Republic in his vision, so he allowed atrocities to be committed by his own people. The actions of these men led to the deaths of thousands of innocent people. In Hitler's case, he killed more than 6 million Jews in order to satisfy his goal.

ALL THESE MEN strove to make their countries into what they wanted them to be. They wanted to fulfill their expectations and goals. But in the pursuit of the fulfillment of their expectations, these men caused great and serious harm to their own people. Hundreds of thousands of people were murdered, massacred, flayed alive, buried alive, slowly drowned, disemboweled, raped, and tortured in the pursuit of their goals.

If a human being performs serious harm to other human beings in the pursuit of fulfilling his expectations, then he has committed great evil. Therefore, expectations can lead a man to evil as easily they can lead him to good, whether positive or negative.

3

TUNNEL-VISION: DARK THOUGHTS.

"Think not lightly of evil, saying, 'It will not come to me.' Drop by drop is the water pot filled. Likewise, the fool, gathering it little by little, fills himself with evil."

— Buddha

What Is Tunnel-Vision?

Tunnel vision is the tendency to consider a preferred line of thought or to focus on something wholly while ignoring everything else. At times, this can be a helpful ability, such as when a surgeon is conducting an operation or when you are trying to survive during a difficult situation. At other times, tunnel-vision can hinder an individual from seeing the full picture because they are too involved in whatever they are doing.

When someone experiences tunnel-vision they neglect important things in favor of urgent things. They prioritize specific things over a slew of other things. There are degrees of tunnel vision and these degrees are associated with prioritization of concerning factors. These factors can range from just being fearful of something to actively neglecting it or ignoring it because it incites fear in the heart of an individual.

A mild example of tunnel vision can be when an individual fears social gatherings and tries to actively avoid them. An obsessive tunnel vision case develops in two ways. Either an individual becomes obsessed about something such as turning violent when being disrespected or they start to neglect mundane priorities such as morals, social activities, hygiene, nutrition, sleep, education or employment in their concern over their obsession.

Many times, the behavior of people with tunnel vision may seem irrational. They may be unapologetic for their behavior towards other people, even their family members. They may neglect or offend their family or friends in pursuit of their goal or concern and may have a hard time understanding why their closest family and friends may not be helping them. They may lash out or say things that alienate people, inadvertently harming themselves due to their obsession.

People deep in the throes of tunnel vision can cheat on their spouses to feel validated, spend hard-earned cash on a whim, become helicopter parents, can sabotage a project so others cannot succeed, end a friendship because some behavior violates their boundaries, or can become violent when their tenants are violated.

Dark thoughts are unwanted, intrusive thoughts, images or ideas that come from nowhere into a person's mind and cause great distress or anxiety. These thoughts are disturbing, taboo, graphic and embarrassing. They usually focus around behaviors which are unacceptable morally or lawfully such as sexual or violent images that are unacceptable or thoughts about harming someone loved by an individual.

Dark thoughts can range from mild to extreme. Extreme forms of dark thoughts can be killing someone, committing suicide, getting revenge, sabotaging someone, cheating, cannibalism, incest, pedophilia, stealing, beating someone up, and taking someone forcefully, among others. They are actually very common. Everyone in their life experiences these thoughts at least once—usually more than a dozen times. They are connected to our dark side. Whenever we feel angry, fearful, or hateful, these thoughts pop up from the unconscious mind.

. . .

These thoughts can feel shameful because they contain disturbing or wretched imaginings that a person would never even think of; however, unless we act on them, these thoughts are just that: *thoughts.* However, these thoughts can become intrusive thoughts if we start to fear them or fixate on them. The greater our fixation or fear, the more power and energy these thoughts gain so they return again and again. This repeat cycle can break down a person's will.

The Ironic Process Theory states that the harder you try to suppress a thought, the more you will think about it. So, trying to stop thinking about these dark thoughts does not work because the more you try to avoid them the more you fixate on them. This fixation can result in a looping of dark thoughts, which can result in a person committing evil or doing serious harm to other people.

In order to banish these thoughts, the best strategy is to face them and ask yourself if a single thought shows who you truly are. It certainly does not. Humans are not defined by a single thought or impulse. They are complex beings. So, a single thought does not represent all of who we are.

Tunnel-Vision and Dark Thoughts: Relation

Tunnel vision and dark thoughts can compound each other. Tunnel vision is the tendency to neglect everything in favor of one thing and dark thoughts are intrusive images, thoughts, or ideas that are distressing. They both combine together and can force a person to do things they never would have thought of doing otherwise. Dark thoughts can make a person become obsessive, and tunnel vision can make a person think dark thoughts.

Consider the example of a man who is working in an office. His team has gotten a project that is extremely important to complete. There is someone in the team who is known as the best worker in the whole company. This is the worker the man has been jealous of for a long time. After working for a while on the project, the man realizes that he will not get the credit for this project. His co-worker will get the credit again.

The man's jealousy heightens. He starts to think about how he could stop the person from receiving the credit. At first, he tries not to do anything. He tries to go on. But then, one day, a coworker comments on how the man himself used to be the best employee in the company until his coworker came. The man's jealousy spills over. He realizes that he was the best until the co-worker came, and he wants to be the best again. When everyone is gone from the office, he sabotages the whole project, setting it back by weeks.

THE MAN'S obsession with being the best at his company fueled dark thoughts which led him to commit a mistake. He actively tried to harm his co-worker's reputation due to his jealousy so they would not get the credit they deserved. He showed malevolent intention towards the co-worker and, therefore, his actions can be classified as evil. Evil actions cause serious, excessive harm to other human beings.

Let's consider another example. Sienna is a lady's maid. She braids, dresses, beautifies, massages, mends clothes, and supports her lady in everything. Sienna has a sweetheart. He tells her that he loves her. He also tells her that her lady must never know of his relationship with her. Sienna realizes that this is true, her lover is the lady's fiancé. They have been engaged to be married since they were born.

One day, Sienna realizes that she is with child. She goes to inform her lover of the fact, and he tells her that she must not tell anybody. So, Sienna does not. A few weeks pass. Then a month. Then another few weeks pass. Sienna gets worried. She goes to her lover again and asks him about his plans. He tells her that he will marry her if the lady is out of the picture. Sienna comes to an average family. She realizes the honor she would get from this marriage. She asks him if she should leave her service. Her lover tells her that for him to marry her, she has to make sure the lady is out of the picture. When he gives her a powder, she realizes what she must do.

Sienna agonizes over the decision for a few days. Then she realizes that her lady has lived a life of privilege since she was born. If Sienna had such a life, her child could grow up happy. Her child matters more to her than the lady she has served since she was fifteen. She also realizes that she could live life like a high-society lady. She mixes the powder into the lady's sleeping tonic and watches as she drinks it. Then Sienna turns off the lamps and goes to sleep. The next day she wakes up to a corpse and starts screaming. She thinks she is free.

Sienna's obsession with her lover drove her to commit murder. She did not think about the consequences of her actions. She didn't think about the likelihood of her lover marrying her if she did this heinous act. She thought about the privilege her lady had had for a lifetime and wanted it for her child and most of all for herself. She did not think about anything but herself when she murdered her lady.

. . .

Both these examples show that in the grip of both dark thought and obsessions, people can commit grievous wrongs. They can become deaf to everything but their purpose and refuse to or cannot comprehend the consequences of their actions. This leads them to make decisions that can be harmful both to other people and to themselves.

Conclusion

Dark thoughts can force humans towards evil and can force them to harm each other. Tunnel vision can make a person blind to wrong things. Both of these can compound the effects of each other and can make a person blind to the wider consequences of their actions. Therefore, if both of these forces work together they have the potential to cause serious harm to human beings.

4

TEMPTATION AND WEAK WILL.

> "Never open the door to a lesser evil, for other and greater ones invariably slink in after it."
>
> — Baltasar Gracian

Lure of Temptation

Temptation is the desire to do something wrong or unwise, something that endangers long-term goals. It is an immediate urge or impulse to do something. It indicates a lack of self-control and is something that allures and excites someone to do something they normally would not do. Temptations can be felt for materialistic goods such as wealth, land, or women and for psychological tenants such as desire, lust, dark thoughts, and other immoral thoughts, among others.

From the religious perspective, temptation is the way that leads to sin. It is the urge that led to the fall of man from heaven (the time when the devil tempted Adam and Eve and they fell for his lie); therefore, it is an urge that can wreak havoc. According to religious scholars, it can cause one to disregard religious beliefs and makes it likely for people to make the wrong decisions. However, at other times, temptation can be looked upon as a gift or an opportunity of growth by the religious people who experience it.

Temptations can range from weak and subtle temptations to strong and obvious temptations. Both types can lead to a loss of self-control, but the stronger temptations lead to a greater loss. Temptations can also have negative and positive consequences. Some people regard temptations as an opportunity for growth because it helps them recognize constructive and destructive behaviors and emotions. Some people regard temptations as negative because they make them consider things which they would not normally do.

At times, temptation can be harmless, such as the temptation for delicious food, beautiful clothes, or handsome tools. At other times it can lead one to evil actions such as the temptation to acquire a beautiful woman, desiring an immoral outcome to something, or wanting to hurt someone.

What Is Weakness of Will?

Weakness of will is essentially the failure to act on a decision or behaving in a way that adheres to moral values. A weak-willed person lacks the strength of will to stand by their decisions. They are easily swayed and can change their decisions, opinions, or plans on a whim. A weak-willed person is someone who knows what is right but chooses to do what is not right. An agent with a weak will does not really know what the best decision is so they vacillate between making one decision in a moment and changing it the next.

Underneath the problem of weakness lies the assumption that a person's judgement about what is best, their desire for what is best, and doing what is actually best are connected. This assumption relies on the fact that an individual knows which course of action is better than the other. It also assumes that evaluative judgements are connected to motivation and hence to action.

Let's consider the example of Sarah, who always wanted to pursue a Ph.D. in biochemistry. When she completes her masters, she revisits this issue, and tries to think what she wants to do. Finally, after a lot of thought she registers in a Ph.D. program. After three months of constant research, she finds that she lacks motivation, is restless, and does not want to finish the degree. But she cannot just give up; she thinks she needs to persevere. And despite her better judgement, she continues. A year later, bitter and hopeless, Sarah finally quits her job. She finally realizes that no matter what she felt, she should have stopped the program before committing so much time and money to it.

Sarah should have quit before she hit rock bottom. She had very good reasons not to pursue a career in biochemistry. She was not thriving in the degree and felt drained and battered. But, in direct contrast to her judgement, she did not stop when she should have. She impulsively, on the basis of her feelings, acted *against* her better judgement when it obviously supported that she should quit the program. She showed a lack of control. She obviously knew what the correct decision was, but she was weak-willed and didn't ascribe to it.

THIS SHOWS that even the most intelligent of people are susceptible to weak will. Weak will is not related to low moral standards. Rather, it is the failure of acting upon an evaluative judgment.

. . .

Let's consider the example of Janet, who takes drugs to alleviate her depression. Janet wasabused during her early childhood and is, as a result, very scarred. She rarely trusts anybody, and she hates men with a passion . Sometimes she has these episodes in which all she feels is fear and terror. Those days are the worst days of her life. She relives everything she went through.

One day, when she's going through one of her episodes, one of her friends brings her something that will relax her. After taking the pill, she does relax and starts to feel good. She even comes out of her room to thank her friend. Her friend, however, is quiet and barely receptive, so Janet returns to her room. A few weeks pass and Janet forgets what she dreamed about that time, but remembers the euphoria vividly.

Then suddenly, her dreams return. She wakes up trembling in fear, her bed wet with sweat. She is shaking uncontrollably. She dimly recalls that last time her friend gave her something that made her dreams better. She knows that it is bad for her. But she just needs enough to stop her dreams. She goes to her friend and tries to beg her for some of those pills. Her friend refuses and tells her that when she gave her the pill the first time, her nightmares were uncontrollable, but today she can walk and talk, so there's no need for them.

JANET BEGS, pleads, and tries everything, but her friend is unmoved. Janet acts out and goes into her room. The rest of her night passes in agony. When she wakes up the day after, she realizes what she was doing was wrong and goes to her friend to apologize. Her friend tells her that she wasn't herself. Janet accepts that and tells her that she is grateful to her friend for not giving her any.

JANET GOES through another few episodes, battling the desire for the drug, until one that she can't resist. It is the worst one yet. Janet wakes up the next day and realizes that *she has to have that drug for emergencies.* She goes and buys some of that drug. A few episodes pass. She does not take the drug. But when a particularly hard one arrives, she does take one. She finds instant relief. Her mood tuns mellow and light. It almost seems like her worries are gone.

Janet realizes that she likes the feeling; however, she cautions herself against the adverse effects of the drug. She holds out for a few months until consecutive episodes leave her screaming in pain. She takes one pill to relieve herself. One then becomes two. Two then become three. Janet finds that she doesn't want to stop anymore.

Janet's example shows that even people with a strong will (the people who follow evaluative judgements) are also susceptible to temptation. Janet knew that taking the drug was bad for her. She held out for months and months, until she couldn't. The temptation was reinforced in her mind by her consecutive episodes. She felt terrible, so she craved the serenity of the drug. She wanted out of her nightmares, so she craved calm.

In the end, the drug offered everything she wanted, and even with all her intelligence, the temptation to take the drug overcame the judgement Janet had already made.

Weak Will and Temptation: The Road to the Dark Side

Weak will and temptation can amplify the effects of each other. Temptation can weaken the will of a person, so they are more susceptible to taking decisions without paying any attention to evaluative judgments. Likewise, a weak will can also make a person submit to temptation easily. A weak-willed person has low self-control, so any temptation is acted upon. Very rarely do these kinds of people stop to consider the consequences of their actions.

Consider the example of a man forced into slavery. The man was a hunter who just happened to be in the way of slavers. He was in the wrong place at the wrong time. The slavers kidnapped him and took him to a slave market to be sold. Declan was sold to a great many masters over the next four years. Some were good to him; some were worse. Many he wished to kill, but could not because they were out of his hand. By the time Declan turned thirty, he had more scars on his body than skin. He had been a particularly errant slave since his bonds were put on him.

DECLAN'S current owner was kind. He fed his slaves well, practiced mercy when they made a mistake, and gave them good clothes. He was a kind-hearted master.. Declan, who had once been a free man, hated him more than all of his previous master's combined. This man pretended to be kind when he had stolen the lives of people. This man pretended to be merciful when no one would begrudge him his right to excise justice. This man turned a blind eye to the injustice being done to the slaves by other masters. Declan thought that no matter how kind a master was, he was still a master.

One day, Declan was doing his tasks when a previous master, a friend of his current master, came to his master's house. The man stopped and looked at Declan for a long moment. Then he said something to the kind master. The kind master refused to do whatever it was.

. . .

So, his older master came every month for the next two years, working on his kind master, who refused his suggestions at every turn. Then the day came when the kind master could not refuse the suggestion of the harsh master, who promised him a vote in the government if the master gave him one day with the slave. The kind master hesitated. A vote to abolish slavery or the life of a slave. There was not even a choice. Afterall, some men had been made to rule and some made to serve. He could not do anything if his slave was the latter.

The harsh man brought his whip, and he brought his chains. He tied Declan up and did heinous things to him. However, midway through the ordeal, the master was called by the kind master to the main house. Whatever happened there is unknown, but while the master was gone, another slave came and undid Declan's bonds. An idea came to Declan, he had resisted killing so many harsh masters just because he thought they had been out of his hand. Today he had a master in reach. He would not let him go, no matter the consequences.

. . .

THEREFORE, when the harsh master came back, Declan hid behind the stable doors, the whip in his hand and waited until the harsh master stepped inside. The moment the master stepped inside the stable, Declan jumped at him and choked him to death with his own whip.

IN THIS EXAMPLE, Declan is enslaved by men who do serious harm to other human beings. No rational human would deny that they are not evil. But, Daniel's actions are also evil. He killed the harsh master with intention. His intent was to harm the task master. His temptation led him to commit an evil action, enough though it could be justified in the eyes of moral law.

Conclusion

In the end, weak will and temptation can amplify each other. Weak will can make temptations alluring and easy to submit to, while constant temptations weaken the will, which can lead to the commission of harmful actions.

5

SOCIAL DISPARITY: EFFECT ON PSYCHE.

"A son, as such, belongs to his father, and a slave, as such, belongs to his master; yet each, considered as a man, is something having separate existence and distinct from others. Hence in so far as each of them is a man, there is justice towards them in a way: and for this reason, too there are certain laws regulating the relations of father to his son, and of a master to his slave; but in so far as each is something belonging to another, the perfect idea of "right" or "just" is wanting to them."

—Thomas Aquinas

Social Disparity: Definitions, Types, and Effects

What Is Social Disparity?

Social disparity, also called social inequality, is the unequal distribution of valued goods and services in a society by a social process. It can be brought about by societal norms that are influenced by power, prestige, religion, nepotism, race, ethnicity, gender, age, sexual orientation, and class. Social disparity can affect the distribution of rights and privileges among a group of people or, at a broader scale, in a society. These social rights can include health care, freedom of speech, education, housing, opportunity, political representation, law, and work opportunities, among others. Many times, it has been linked to racial inequality, gender inequality, status inequality, and income inequality, as well as other social statuses.

. . .

According to Hradil (2001:30), "Social inequality exists when people frequently receive more of a society's 'valuable goods' than others owing to their position in the social network of relationships." This definition says that differences in physical features cannot be called social differences because they are not the end product of a social process. It also says that social disparity is defined by an individual's parents' social class or economic status, and it effects the individual's social class and economic status.

Social disparity is found in almost every single existing and past society. It can be shaped by dozens of factors, such as cultural norms, class difference, citizenship status, and geographical locations. In simple societies, such as nomadic societies, social disparity may be very low because the daily life of those in power may be similar to those not in power, goods and services may be distributed equally between the society, and gender roles may also be equal. This relatively low social disparity may result from the kinship-oriented structure of the society, which values social harmony more than wealth or status. However, this type of society may fail to develop because the culture may actively work towards reducing conflict, which is a cornerstone of the development of societies.

In stratified societies, where classification is done by capitalizing on the differences between wealth, power, prestige, and status, individuals are ranked into classes such as upper class, middle class, and lower or working class. The upper class consists of the leaders of the society or those who are influential, while the lower class consist of those who do menial jobs or those who lack wealth, prestige, or power. Social status in these societies is passed down from one generation to another. Stratified societies can be found all throughout history, such as the kingdoms of France, England, Portugal, and Spain over the centuries.

The so-called dimensions of social inequality state that some goods contribute to social inequality because they are in high demand amongst the society and unequally distributed. These goods can be material wealth, power, prestige, education, working conditions, housing, environmental and leisure conditions, social capital, security, and mobility. According to Hradil (20021:34), "The determinants of social inequality denote social positions of individuals in networks of social relations [...]; these positions do not represent advantages or disadvantages as such but very likely produce them." In simple words, he says that the distribution of these "goods" governs the social status or situation of the individual and may produce inevitable advantages or disadvantages for the individual.

CONSIDER the case of a nobleman who was born into an old and wealthy family. He has had the best education growing up. He also has power, prestige, and immense wealth. Everything was given to him at birth. Similarly, let's consider the case of a boy born into the slums of the city to a prostitute. This boy has never had the education or housing conditions the noble has, nor does he have the social mobility the noble has. The boy's station produces disadvantages for him. Thus, the determinants of social inequality govern what kind of life he will have. In the nobleman's case, there are a number of advantages produced for him by his station. But in the boy's case, there are a number of disadvantages produced for him by his station. These extreme examples show that the division of "goods and services" in a society governs the social position of an individual and most likely produces advantages and disadvantages for them.

THESE EXAMPLES SHOW that social disparity undermines social justice and human rights and the connected nature of inequalities shows that some groups have consistently worse opportunities when compared to their fellow citizens.

TYPES OF SOCIAL Disparity

THERE ARE five types of social disparity, such as wealth disparity, political disparity, life (or opportunity) disparity, treatment disparity, and membership inequality. Social Disparity can be applied to both individuals and to societies; however, in this chapter, we will only talk about the effects of social disparity on individuals.

1. **Political Disparity:** Political disparity shows the differences between civic inequality and the inequality of law between persons and societies. It is brought about by the inability of some individuals or races, castes, ethnicities, and religions to access governmental resources; they may not have the power to influence political decision and outcomes. For example, women were not allowed to vote even though they were an important part of society.

2. **Wealth and Income Disparity**: Wealth disparity is the unequal distribution of assets such as property, capital, investments, businesses, and valuables, among others. Income disparity is the extent to which income is distributed unevenly between a group of people. For example, in the United States, the top 0.1% of the population has wealth beyond measure, while the rest of the population does not.

. . .

3. **Life or Opportunity Disparity**: Life or opportunity disparity takes root when not every citizen of a society is entitled to a decent start in life. This means that some people do not have the same opportunities in life that other people have due to their ascribed characteristics (qualities given at birth or by others such as physical characteristics, sex, social status of parents, etc.) or achieved characteristics (earned or chosen characteristics such as education, merit, etc.)

4. **Treatment Disparity**: Treatment disparity occurs when some individuals or races, castes, ethnicities, and religions can benefit more and receive more privileges than others. For example, some employed people are given more responsibilities and receive more compensation and benefits for the same type of work as their counterparts with the same qualifications.

5: **Membership Disparity**: Membership disparities occur when individuals or groups of people, either due to their caste, religion, ethnicity, or race, are not accepted as a member of a community, a group, a family or a household. For example, black people were not allowed into universities or even neighborhoods because they were deemed as different or dangerous by white people.

Effects of Social Inequality.

Social inequality can result in bigotry, prejudice, xenophobia, discrimination, exclusion, and persecution, among others, towards individuals, or a certain race, caste, religion, or ethnicity, in a society. These psychological mechanisms are associated with negative outcomes, such as lower happiness, lower social cohesion, weaker morality, lower life satisfaction, higher mortality, worse health, and weaker governance.

According to Ostry et al., 2014, inequality "can undermine the progress in health and education, cause investment reducing political and economic instability, and undercut the social consensus required to adjust in the face of major shocks, and thus... it tends to reduce the pace and durability of growth." In fact, inequality can negatively affect growth because it incites a society to make efforts to redistribute through the tax system, which in turn effects growth considerably.

Living in highly unequal societies can increase mistrust and status competition, both of which have harmful effects on the health and well-being of an individual. People who mistrust their fellow people believe that the economy is unfair and that others are advancing themselves by questionable means. This mistrust undermines social connection and civility and so these individuals believe that the perceived immoral behavior of other people allows them to take morally ambiguous actions to get the things they want.

Status competition can stem from the fears of losing one's standing or from how others perceive it. People may start to think that by displaying high standing people could only have a sense of self. They may become obsessed with status hierarchy and may do actions that are not morally acceptable or motivated by moral agents.

SOCIAL INEQUALITY RESULTS in the want for material wealth because the disadvantaged think, incorrectly, that they have been deprived of this wealth due to their status or unequal distribution. Similarly, the advantaged individuals think to preserve their own material wealth in fear that it would be taken away from them. This suggests that material wealth is central to the analysis of social inequality because in modern societies material wealth is necessary for a high standard of living because it can buy material goods and immaterial goods such as security, health, etc., to a large extent.

ACCORDING TO GEORGE BERNARD SHAW, "The lack of money is the root of all evil." Money is central to social inequality because in today's societies it is necessary to have money if an individual wants a reasonable standard of life. Money can buy both tangible goods such as housing, and employment, but it can also buy intangible goods such as health, security, etc., to a very large extent. It can provide safety to someone who does not have it. As mentioned above, social disparity creates problems. It undermines social mobility, creates prejudice and xenophobia, and strips people of their human and social rights. Significant social disparity combined with desperation can make paths that seemed morally prohibited seem like paths of redemption. Individuals in their mistrust can commit actions that can be labeled as evil.

Social Disparity and the Dark Side

As mentioned above, social disparity can cause problems in a society and can limit growth. It can provide advantages to some individuals, while providing the opposite to others. It can result in lack of social mobility, persecution, discrimination, and prejudice towards an individual, or a group, caste, religion, race or ethnicity. Individuals can be stripped of their social and human rights when they undergo the effects of social disparity. These foregone rights can include limited or no access to education and healthcare, access to housing, employment, and political and moral rights, among others.

Social disparity can breed mistrust among the people of a society or a regime. When nothing is done for them, the people may start to think that society deliberately keeps them disadvantaged. This may create social instability, which may in turn halt economic development. They may start rebellions—which can destroy infrastructure, kill and massacre those who they perceive to be their wrongdoers, and commit atrocities.

Consider the example of the mob of Paris during the French Revolution. The mob was granted its power by Robespierre—the man who found the Terror himself. It consisted of the dregs of the social classes; the people who had toiled and struggled for every ingot and penny they ever got. There were prostitutes, grave diggers, latrine cleaners, beggars, and thieves, among others, in the mob. They had seen the noble and high classes studiously ignore them for centuries. They had seen injustices done against them with no one the wiser.

They had struggled and struggled for everything, while the ones who called themselves their betters lounged about on their divans and drank cold wine in the sweltering weather.

THESE PEOPLE HAD BEEN PERSECUTED, discriminated, been the target of hate and disgust, had no social mobility or equality, and had no human rights under any law. They saw the propaganda against the nobility and high classes and realized that they may have a chance to avenge their wrongs. So, they did. All the hatred, persecution, bigotry, xenophobia, disgust, and other phycological impacts they had been through boiled over. The mob of Paris disemboweled people, ripped their arms off when they were alive, cannibalized them, buried people alive, cheered and insulted those on the guillotine, and murdered enough people to warrant them a stay in hell.

THEY KILLED because they had suffered, and they found joy in hurting those who they thought had made them suffer. They killed without remorse and committed atrocities that would make saner people shriek with terror.

They did inhumane acts, and they vented out their rage, which had been trapped inside them for decades.

The mob didn't do this slaughter suddenly, without any motive, rather, they had been the victims of social disparity and they lashed out when provided the chance.

Conclusion.

Social disparity is a social phenomenon which can lead to the degradation of human and social rights of people, such as judicial access, freedom of speech, education, housing, and work opportunities, among others. It can hinder the economic growth of a society and can cause devastating effects on the psychological mindset of an individual or a society as a whole. It can lead to the start of persecution, bigotry, discrimination, and other psychological mechanisms that can sever groups of people from each other. Therefore, social disparity is something that can lead to evil if it is let go freely.

6

IGNORANCE: FEIGNED OR REAL.

"The world is a dangerous place to live, not because of the people who are evil, but because of the people who don't do anything about it."

— Albert Einstein

Ignorance is the state of being uninformed. It is the willful neglect or refusal to acquire knowledge. Ignorance can be deliberate and conscious or inadvertent and unconscious. Ignorance usually excuses an individual from responsibility of their actions, unless they are culpable for the ignorance itself.

IGNORANCE CAN APPEAR in three types: factual ignorance—the absence of knowledge of a fact; objectual ignorance—unfamiliarity with an object, and technical ignorance—not knowing how to do something. Moral theology also divides ignorance into many categories, two of which are: vincible and invincible ignorance. Vincible ignorance is ignorance that can be overcome if an effort is made to acquire knowledge. Invincible ignorance is ignorance that could not be removed even after applying as much diligence as possible.

AN EXAMPLE of invincible ignorance could be this: a birthday party was going on and some boys, in their excitement, planned to hit their friend in his face with the cake. When their friend blew out the candles, his friends tried to slam his head into the cake, but they ended up hitting it on the thick wooden table. The boy fell down unconscious, a dent in his forehead. Later, they learned that the boy may not survive as a result of their prank. The boys committed an action that they could not have been aware of beforehand, no matter how much they tried to know about it.

All of humanity is ignorant to a certain point and is different in its willingness to cling to it or move away from it. Individuals could be ignorant of different things, for example that their conduct has a certain outcome, or that they could act otherwise. Moreover, they may be ignorant in different ways. They might never have considered the issue, or they might have considered it, but be mistaken about it.

Consider the example of NRA, the National Rifle Association in the USA, which insists that gun control (or the lack of it) is not the problem behind mass shootings. They believe that the culprit behind mass shooting is some mental issue, It is obvious that those behind the mass shootings have a mental problem, but so does the NRA by refusing to face the reality that by making gun purchases easily accessible to anybody, they are facilitating these acts. They are clinging to their ignorance position in order to show their righteousness, but in fact they are facilitating evil in their ignorance. They are unaware of the harm they are causing in their ignorance.

As shown by the example above, ignorance can have negative effects on individuals and societies. In this case, the lax rules of the NRA are making it easier for mentally unstable individuals to purchase guns. However, ignorance can also have positive effects on both individuals and societies because it makes things clearer and steers away from evil actions. It can also light up the desire to seek more knowledge within individuals. Therefore, it is the moral duty of every human to move away from ignorance by building upon their knowledge to travel towards a path of wisdom.

Debate on Ignorance

Ignorance and Evil

As Socrates once pointed out twenty-five-hundred years ago, ignorance is the ultimate evil. He believed that no one does wrong voluntarily. Evil is the result of ignorance. If people knew what the right thing to do was, they would do it. Humanity has always chosen what it thought was the best or good for it. So, if an individual chooses to do what other people think is wrong, then that individual must have made a mistake and should be educated to see the error. They mistook evil for good.

SOCRATES' theory was that an evildoer knows that other people think of his actions as wrong, but he does not believe it himself. The evildoer thinks that there is something good for him in the evil act, so he does it. Socrates believed that if the evil person just understood what they had done they would never do it again. He therefore argues that overcoming ignorance is necessary for self-knowledge and the good life.

PROCLUS SUPPORTS SOCRATES VIEW, he states that, "Evil, (. . .), we say is wanted (abouleuton) by nobody, and to those who choose it, evil seems to be a good. For no soul would knowingly choose evil, but would avoid it. Due to ignorance, however, [the soul] is occupied with it. For although it has by nature a 'keen love' of the good, it is unable to see where the good lies." In simple words, he says that everyone desires good but due to ignorance individuals unwillingly surrender themselves to moral error and evil. He believes that evil is involuntary and results from ignorance.

He further states, "For all things are for the sake of this good, all the good and all the contrary things alike. Indeed, when we act badly, we do so out of ignorance as to the nature of these deeds, despite desire for the good. [. . .] Therefore, evil is often said to be involuntary. Indeed, how could it be voluntary if it is done for the sake of the good, whereas according to what it actually is, it is that which is neither desirable to, nor willed by, any being?"

Proclus highlights how ignorance leads an individual to act contrary to their will. In his Commentary on the Alcibiades I, he recognizes the difference between forms of ignorance, with some being excusable because they do not harm the soul while others being inexcusable because they harm the soul and may forever doom us to evil. He regards excusable ignorance as *simple ignorance,* in which an individual recognizes the ignorance in their soul and seeks out the knowledge they lack. The latter he regards as double ignorance or the ignorance of ignorance combined with moral pretense i.e., pretending to be knowledgeable, in which the individual harbors the false assumption that "one knows when one does not"; they are conceited, and believe that they know everything there is to know.

Consider the example of Emily, a woman who sees locked-up men and women in a prison. She is a rebel. She infiltrates into the jail as a spy and finds a horrifying spectacle before her eyes. She finds half-starved men and women who look like hollows of their former selves. She finds fellow rebels who look like skeletons. She works for a while at the jail and when she gets a chance, she releases those prisoners, burning with the desire to free them, not thinking about what will happen to them when they get out, or when someone catches them.

. . .

Emily releases the prisoners, but unbeknownst to her, several days later nearly every single freed prisoner dies at the hands of the police force and the people who are out for them. Barely anyone survives.

Emily's actions suggest that she never even thought about what would happen to them. She acted from a well of ignorance. Should she be responsible for her actions? Did she permit the deaths?

Aristotle argues that acts done through ignorance of particulars, not acts done through ignorance of universals, are non-voluntary. Because when acts done from ignorance of particulars are caused by ignorance, they are excused. In the case of Emily, she is ignorant of a particular cause; she is ignorant of "to what end" she acts. She thinks that she is saving the greatest number of lives possible, when in fact, she is letting someone die unnecessarily. She could have had a better plan, but she did not. She didn't focus on the particulars, nor did she dwell on them.

. . .

Is she evil because she let people die unnecessarily in her ignorance? If she had informed herself properly, would she still be culpable for her actions and her ignorance about what would happen?

There are two rival views on this question. Volitionism says that we are culpable for our ignorance only if we were aware that we had to inform ourselves better, while attributionism says that we are culpable whenever our ignorance is due to a lack of moral concern. If evil actions lack morality and cause excessive, serious harm to other human beings, then is Emily evil?

It can be said that someone like Emily is not blameworthy because she did not act viciously . However, at times, the morally ignorant do act viciously. For example, they may act with epistemic vices—intellectual dispositions such as character traits and mental skills, which are in their control.

. . .

Immanuel Kant's Deontology theory says that to determine if an act is right or wrong, we have to consider the intention, motivation, or principle for which the agent acts. Emily probably acted on a principle that most of us can get behind—the principle that she should save as many lives as possible. She chose her plan because she thought that it would save as many lives as possible. Therefore, if Deontology is true, then Emily is not guilty of a failure to realize that putting the plan into motion may have been morally wrong because it is not even wrong to begin with.

For Deontologists, if an individual acts from ignorance on a bad moral principle and does something wrong, their ignorance is essentially moral ignorance, which is culpable. If one acts from ignorance about a factual claim, but also acts on a principle that one can get behind, then the act is not wrong to begin with.

Conclusion.

Ignorance that is vincible may entitle an individual to be punished for their actions, as it could have been removed by the pursuit of knowledge, however, invincible ignorance does the opposite because the actions that took place could not have been foreseen by the wrongdoer, even if they put all the resources they had to finding the knowledge. Therefore, ignorance can lead to an individual committing evil acts because of their lack of knowledge. The extent of the punishment for their actions depends on how much effort the individual put into removing their ignorance.

7

HURT AND ANGER: THE ROAD TO REVENGE AND RETRIBUTION.

"If you prick us, do we not bleed? if you tickle us, do we not laugh? if you poison us, do we not die? and if you wrong us, shall we not revenge?"

— William Shakespeare

Anger and Hurt: The Road to Evil

Anger is an intense emotion that is inversely related to hurt and fear. When considered positive, it is viewed as a protective response towards a perceived threat. When considered negative, it is known as aggression. It is a psychological defense that, while protecting our ego, makes far more problems than it solves. Anger is classified as one of the primary emotions but often is not a primary feeling ; there are many hurt emotions lying underneath it, such as feeling guilty, rejected, powerless, devalued, unimportant, disregarded, and accused, among others. These feelings generate incredible emotional pain, which is why most individuals try their hardest to distance themselves from them by using anger as a shield.

According to the cognitive consistency theory, anger can be caused by an inconsistency between an expected or desired outcome and the actual outcome of an event. This makes the angry individual react in order to reduce inconsistency. An angry person may lose their empathy, thoughtfulness, and objectivity and may cause harm to themselves or others. Anger can also influence aggression and can increase its intensity or probability. It can be expressed negatively, through frustration, intimidation to meet our own needs, and hostility or over-protective instinct, which is used to avoid the loss of something.

ANGER CAN COME in three forms: passive, aggressive, and assertive.

1. **Passive Anger:** Passive anger can be expressed through actions such as giving someone the cold shoulder, avoiding conflict, becoming obsessive, manipulating people, giving the silent treatment, and emotional blackmail.

2. **Aggressive Anger:** Aggressive anger can be expressed through actions such as threatening, insulting, shouting at, and persecuting people; destroying objects and relationships; talking over people, being violent, breaking promises, blaming, using foul language, verbal abuse, labelling others, being selfish, frightening people, and being vengeful.

. . .

3. **Assertive Anger:** Assertive anger can be expressed through blaming, calling a person out on their behavior, and punishing them.

ANGER IS a shield that an individual dons when they feel extremely hurt, upset, or fearful. When an individual gets angry, the human body thinks that it is in danger, so it secretes adrenaline—the hormone that makes the individual hyper-vigilant, feel stronger, and ready to do battle. In most cases, the provocation is not related to imminent physical harm at all, rather it is related to the preservation of a person's ego. And the more secure a person's sense of self is, the less they get angry. So, getting angry or furious at feeling vulnerable can be a result of a fragile ego.

SUPPOSE that a wife says something to her husband that makes him feel awful, disregarded, and rejected. But, rather than sharing his feelings with his wife and making himself feel more vulnerable, he attacks her and says petty and cruel things—anything he can remember, no matter how petty—to her.

. . .

Because the husband felt disregarded and hurt, he lashed out at his wife and tried to hurt *her* feelings, to make her feel what he felt. He shakes off his hurt feelings in order to make her feel hurt. The consequence of this action is that now the wife also feels what the husband was feeling. His feelings of hurt have transferred onto the wife. Her response is unpredictable, she may retaliate by saying petty or cruel things back at her husband, or try to defend herself, or walk away from the scene altogether. None of these self-protective urges help the wife understand what triggered the husband's anger. She thinks that her husband just meant her harm, and reacts accordingly.

This example shows that anger rarely resolves anything. Rather, it can aggravate things. According to Mark Twain, "Anger is an acid that can do more harm to the vessel in which it is stored than to anything on which it is poured." He seems to be correct. An individual in the throes of anger can destroy relationships, harmony, and trust, because they try to alleviate their feelings of hurt, fear, guilt on another person rather than talking to them like an adult. Anger can also harm a person's self-esteem; It can make them say or do things that they will regret later. Uncontrolled anger has also been shown to damage a person's health and life expectancy because it elevates blood pressure, increases the heart rate, and triggers the body's fight or flight response.

ANGER CAUSES A REDUCTION IN AN INDIVIDUALS' cognitive and information-processing ability. This reduction in cognitive capacity can cause angry individuals to make risky decisions. Anger makes people less trusting and makes them think negatively about other people or outsiders. Angry people are also more likely to blame a person's actions not on their circumstance but on their nature; they show correspondence bias. They are also more likely to blame another person for their misery. They may also be desirous of an object to which their anger is tied.

SO, how can anger lead to a person commit evil?

. . .

Since it has been mentioned above that anger reduces cognitive capacity, then it is easy to infer that angry people make decisions that are more likely to harm than help them. They make choices while they are angry that might lead them to do things that they had not wanted to do in the first place. They might yearn to take revenge on the person who angered them, and it is this revenge that can get them into trouble. They may commit an immoral action with a malicious intention that could be labeled as evil because it might cause serious, excessive harm to another fellow human being.

> "Holding anger is a poison. It eats you from inside. We think that hating is a weapon that attacks the person who harmed us. But hatred is a curved blade. And the harm we do, we do to ourselves."
>
> — Mitch Albom

What is Revenge?

Revenge is an act of harming or damaging another individual in response to a perceived or real harm or damage, especially resentfully or vindictively. The nature of revenge causes someone to act upon anger rather than reason. People are motivated to seek revenge — to harm someone who has harmed them — when they feel attacked, mistreated or socially rejected.. They are motivated to seek revenge out of a sense of fairness because if an injustice has been committed, then the only way for the slate to become clean is for the wrongdoers to pay for their crimes. Only then does justice prevail. Getting an eye for an eye is said to bring a sense of catharsis and closure to the victim. It may seem brutal at first. However, getting an eye for an eye *limits* the revenge so the justice is proportionate to the injustice. There is no need to take further revenge. That should be the end of the matter. The problem arises when people still yearn to unleash more suffering on the wrongdoer.

Ian Mckee, a social psychologist in his paper *Social Justice Research* says that, "People who are more vengeful tend to be those who are motivated by power, by authority and by the desire for status. They don't want to lose face". In short, this means that the desire for power motivates people to take revenge.

THERE ARE two types of revenge: revenge as punishment and revenge as suffering. There is a vast difference between revenge as suffering and revenge as punishment. Plato in his *Protagoras* says that, "..One who undertakes to punish rationally does not do so for the sake of the wrongdoing, which is now in the past—but for the sake of the future, that the wrongdoing shall not be repeated, either by him {,} or by others who see him {,} or by others who see him punished". To make it clear, Plato is saying that punishment does not have to stem from anger, rather it can just be done in order to right a wrong. This means that while revenge is nearly always motivated by anger and the need to make the wrongdoer suffer, punishment does not need to be.

EARLY PSYCHOLOGICAL VIEWS suggested that revenge provided emotional catharsis. That it made the havoc-wreaking emotions in the slighted one diminish. However, after conducting a few studies, researchers found that the opposite is actually true . Revenge does not provide catharsis, rather it aggravates the emotions of the slighted one. Dr. Kevin Carlsmith of Colgate found out that punishers do not just feel bad about their actions, they think about their actions and may feel worse than those who cannot avenge the wrong. Dr. Carlsmith says that," Those who don't have a chance to take revenge are forced, in a sense, to move on and focus on something different. And they feel happier."

HOWEVER, if most people fail to feel good after taking revenge that does not mean that revenge can never feel good. Mario Gollwitzer, a German psychological scientist explored two theories for the reasons why revenge could be satisfying. The first one "comparative suffering" states that simply seeing the wrongdoer suffer for their actions restores an emotional balance to the victims. While the second one the "understanding hypothesis" states that the wrongdoer's suffering is not enough to satisfy revenge. Instead, the avenger must be reassured that the wrongdoer has understood their actions.

Gollwitzer found that revenge could only succeed when the wrongdoer understood why vengeance occurred. He found that revenge that remained unacknowledged was worse than undertaking the revenge; it provided no satisfaction. His study concluded that revenge is more than payback, it is about delivering a message. If the message is not delivered, then the revenge has not cleaned the slate. This means that revenge might not be about responding to a particular wrongdoing, rather it may be about preventing other wrongdoing from happening.

Conclusion

It is crucial to understand the cause or causes of our anger and the effects of venting out the emotion itself because anger is more destructive than it is helpful. It can harm people irrevocably because in anger individuals utter words which can render their victims helpless, disregarded, and demeaned. Revenge is the same; it gives one no satisfaction to take revenge when it is not acknowledged—when the wrong that was done hasn't been acknowledged. Francis Bacon once said, "In taking revenge, a man is but even with his enemy; but in passing it over, he is superior; for it is a prince's part to pardon." Revenge may not be sweet, but it is not bitter either; however, it would be better for all of us when slapped on one cheek, to turn the other because we do not' know what we would do in our need for vengeance.

PATH TO REDEMPTION.

IS THERE ANY FORGIVENESS FOR THOSE WHO COMMIT EVIL ACTIONS? WHAT IF YOU ARE FORGIVEN, HOW DO YOU CONTROL YOURSELF?

In this section, we will discuss the chance of forgiveness for wrongdoers, the emotional passions that one should avoid in order to pursue good, and the role of guilt, regret, and anger in forgiveness. Lastly, we will discuss the reason why peace can help a wrongdoer.

1

SEVERITY OF ACTIONS: SHADES OF FORGIVENESS.

"A true repentance shuns the evil itself, more than the external suffering or the shame."

—William Shakespeare

AN INEVITABLE FACT OF LIFE IS THAT HUMANS are often mistreated by others. Countless generations of humanity have been hurt by their families, close friends, enemies, and colleagues, among others. From the time of the ancient Greeks to present day, forgiveness has been regarded as either a response that is meted out to someone who has wronged or injured another person or as an absolution that is sought by those who have wronged someone else. One thing everyone agrees on is that forgiveness is entirely personal to the giver; it cannot be enforced nor can it be given without thought.

FORGIVENESS IS a moral virtue that is a matter of the heart, the inner self, and involves a change in inner feelings in the heart of the wronged party towards the wrongdoer. The change in feeling entails overcoming, on moral grounds, the intense negative reactive emotions—resentment, anger, hatred, and the desire for revenge—that naturally come to surface when one has been wronged by a person. It happens when the victim stops feeling resentment or hatred towards their wrongdoer. A person who has forgiven has overcome these vindictive attitudes for a morally creditable motive, such as being moved by the repentance done by the person who wronged us. Usually, such a change in feelings leads to a change of behavior such as reconciliation, but it does not always do so.

. . .

However, it is important to distinguish forgiveness from other responses to wrong-doing with which forgiveness is often confused, such as justification, excuse, pardon, mercy, and reconciliation. Although these concepts can bleed into one another, it is best to get a clear picture of forgiveness by separating them.

Forgiveness and Its Confusion With Other Norms

Justification

Many times, there are some actions taken by us that seem morally wrong. Suppose a man sees another man walk into a store, take an apple, and walk out. The man, seeing this behavior, stalks the apple thief and corners him. He then berates him for stealing the apple. When he is done, the apple-thief tells the man that he owns the store and that he has not stolen anything. The supposed apple-thief has provided a justification for his actions and has stated that no matter what his actions seemed like they were perfectly morally permissible.

THEREFORE, when conduct is justified, it is not morally wrong, but when it is forgiven, then it may be morally wrong. When we regard conduct as justified, such as self-defense, we claim that the stated conduct, through morally wrong was the right thing to do.

EXCUSE

SOMETIMES HUMANS DO things that are actually morally bad but for which they aren't morally blameworthy because they can present excusing conditions against the wrong actions which can make the wrong actions seem not wrong. We can present facts or context about the incident that can show why we thought the course we chose was the right course, even if it was morally wrong.

Simply, to regard conduct as excused is to admit that the conduct was wrong but to claim that the person who engaged in the conduct lacked substantial capacity to conform his conduct to the relevant norms and thus was not fully responsible agent.

When conduct is excused, the wrongdoer is *not* held morally responsible for their conduct. But when one is forgiven for their conduct, they are held responsible for their actions. A necessary condition for forgiveness is that the wrongdoer should be held morally responsible for their conduct.

Mercy

Mercy is a less harsh consequence than the legal law that is afforded to a person who has committed a wrong. It is less personal than forgiveness, since the person granting mercy will not be a victim of wrongdoing and will not have any feeling of resentment to overcome. There is a clear difference between forgiveness and mercy: mercy is typically given by third-parties, while forgiveness is given directly by the victim to the wrongdoer. Mercy is also overly given, while forgiveness can be given both overtly and privately. Mercy can be given by third-parties, but forgiveness cannot—it is personal to the victim. Lastly, mercy is usually linked to authority as its typically given by someone in a position of authority. Forgiveness, on the other hand, comes under no authority structures.

Reconciliation

When a victim is wronged, the relationship between the wrongdoer and the victim is damaged, possibly irreparably. Minor wrongdoings can strain relationships, but major wrongdoings can shatter them wholly. Blaming the wrongdoer can make this chasm wider, often causing further damage.

Forgiveness is the change in feeling in a victim's heart that prompts them to set aside their anger, resentment, and hatred towards the wrongdoer. Reconciliation is the act of reconstructing or rejoining relationships broken by offences given previously. There is a vast difference between both of them, but since forgiveness often leads to reconciliation, it is easy to confuse both concepts.

It is necessary to understand that forgiveness is a helpful step towards reconciliation, but it is not a necessary condition for reconciliation. Reconciliation can happen without granting forgiveness. After all, reconciliation can be adopted for instrumental reasons, such as maintaining peace and order, keeping a job, working with family, etc. Delaying reconciliation until forgiveness has taken place may make some kinds of reconciliation impossible. Likewise, forgiveness can be granted without reconciliation. This can also happen for many reasons, one being that the wrongdoer may not wish to resume relations with the victim.

Therefore, while at times reconciliation goes hand-in-hand with forgiveness, it is not necessary for granting someone forgiveness.

People who advocate quick forgiveness have a tendency to treat resentment and other vindicative emotions as if they were inherently evil—emotions that no decent and sane person should acknowledge. They enforce that forgiveness should be given to all, regardless of the victim's own feelings. They believe that it is in this time that forgiveness has an important part to play, but they fail to understand the offering of forgiveness without acknowledgment of transgressions. One cannot exist without the other.

These people fail to keep in mind that the problem with vindicative emotions is not that they are evil or bad, it is that they have a tendency to get out of control—to dominate the life of a wronged person so much that they spiral out of control and start revenge seeking. This out-of-control person may start to pose a danger to the very moral and legal order that identifies them as a victim of immorality. A great many times, a victimized person may allow these emotions to take over turning them into a self-righteous fanatic who is so selfishly absorbed by their outrage that they may only be satisfied with the utter annihilation of their transgressor. Such a person may be willing to destroy anyone who gets in the way of his path, even those who have done him no wrong—those who are innocent.

SUCH A PERSON IS a danger to morality and decency of the social order because they can often unconsciously use the language of justice and crime control as rationalization of their sadism and cruelty. Against such a background forgiveness can be seen as a healing balm, something that brings with it a great number of blessings. It has the capacity to free the victim from their anger, their capacity to commit cruelty, and opens the door towards restoration of self and of relationships that are closed to them in their rage.

THIS LAST BLESSING can mean the most to people because it reassures them that when they do something wrong—which is inevitable for humanity—they may still have a way to come back to those they love.

. . .

A VICTIM DOES NOT SUFFER an injury that can be healed easily. They do not suffer a wound that would scar and fade away in time. When people are wronged, they are injured not because of the actions of the wrongdoer but rather by the message the wrongdoer sends to them in their actions; the message that the victim is of less worth than the wrongdoer, that the victim is so unworthy that the wrongdoer may use them as a means to an end or an object in service to their desires or projects.

ACCORDING TO MURPHY AND HAMPTON, the grant of forgiveness must be compatible with self-respect, respect for others as moral agents, and respect for the rules of morality and the moral order. This opinion shows that not resenting or forgiving the wrongdoer hastily gives the message that the victim thought the wrongdoer's actions right—that the actions they committed were correct morally and legally in the victim's eyes. This can damage the standing of the victim.

. . .

However, if the wrongdoer sincerely repents for their actions, if they repudiate their insulting message then the failure to resent or granting forgiveness hastily may be something that would not damage moral and judicial laws. This shows that repentance is necessary for moral forgiveness, and atonement—apology, penance, repentance, etc.—should be made by the wrongdoer towards the victim.

But why should a wrongdoer repent for their actions in order to be forgiven? Why should-forgiveness not be given to a person before they have a change of heart? One, because it is commonly thought forgiveness granted in the absence of apology and repentance can show that the wrongdoing was not taken seriously enough by the victim. If the victim gives up their resentment, but the wrongdoer still stands by their disparaging message, then in reality we are condoning the wrongdoing. Two, because such forgiveness indicates a lack of self-respect. This shows that the victim underestimates their own worth and fails to take the effects of the act on them seriously.

. . .

Therefore, a victim cannot forgive their wrongdoer at the cost of their sense of self and their relationships. If a victim forgives their wrongdoer hastily or fails to resent them for their actions, then they may inadvertently send the message that they approve of the wrongdoer's actions.

Conclusion

A man can forgive his offending agent without reconciling with him, and the offender can do the opposite without ever forgiving him. Forgiveness is the ability of a person to let go of resentment and other vindicative emotions that can lead a person towards dangerous paths. Forgiveness may not solve all the problems a victim has, nor should it be enforced upon a person who feels that they cannot forgive their transgressor, but it can prevent the victim from breaking the same moral and legal laws that were broken by their wrongdoer.

2

DON'TS: VICTIM SYNDROME AND MARTYR COMPLEX.

"To those who abuse: the sin is yours, the crime is yours, and the shame is yours. To those who protect the perpetrators: blaming the victims only masks the evil within, making you as guilty as those who abuse. Stand up for the innocent or go down with the rest."

— Flora Jessop

VICTIM SYNDROME AND MARTYR COMPLEX: DEFINITIONS AND EFFECTS

Victim Syndrome

> Self-pity is easily the most destructive of the non-pharmaceutical narcotics; it is addictive, gives momentary pleasure and separates the victim from reality.
>
> —John Gardner

Victim syndrome is a complex in which a person thinks that they are the victims of the negative actions of others without any evidence of such circumstances. As strange as it may sound, these people are victims by choice. And due to this, they may find themselves willingly victimized. These people always complain about "bad things" that happen to them. They believe that they have no control over the way events unfold, and feel like they don't carry responsibility for them. Adolf Eichmann, in the Nuremberg Trials, expressed similar statements. He said that he was powerless to act because he got orders from above. He couldn't have done anything, so he didn't carry any responsibility. He acted like a victim when he was actually the perpetrator of the Holocaust, all in the name of getting out of standing up for his crimes.

THESE PEOPLE CAN PRESENT themselves as victims at one moment and can then become victimizers themselves in another by hurting the people who are trying to help them, leaving them frustrated and confused. People with victim-mentality display passive-aggressive characteristics when interacting with others, such as subtle and indirect ways of getting what they want. They always behave like victims and blame others when bad things happen to them. Their world is populated by victims, victimizers, and a few rescuers. They have an extremely fatalistic outlook on life because, as stated before, they believe that they have no control over the way events unfold. Every negative outcome in their life is due to some person or circumstance beyond their control. Whenever someone tries to help these people, their advice is brushed off by a huge arsenal of reasons why something will not work. They think that their problems are unique and thus unsolvable. They invite people to help them and then turn these people's efforts against them by claiming that those efforts are hurting them.

CONSIDER the example of a criminal who has been in and out jail for over a decade and has been released on parole countless times through that time. Whenever this man comes out of jail, he speaks about his woes and how nothing goes right and how everyone hates him. The problem with this man is that he generates situations in which he inevitably becomes victimized. He picks bar fights and gets thrashed. He leers at women, but when people warn him about his attitude, he expresses confusion. This man is a classic example of man with a victim syndrome. He thinks that everybody in the world is out to get him—that everyone does bad things to him because they dislike him. He generates situations in which he gets hurt and then he complains that he has no control over them. He blames others for everything.

The blame game exhibited by this criminal is an integral part of the victims' modus operandi. Although most of the time their own actions land them in situations that are hard to get out of, they still blame others and find excuses as to why things did not work out, for example, by guilt tripping people and emotionally blackmailing them. They can cheat, lie, sulk, pout, and withdraw from others to make their point and to prove themselves right. They have the knack to drag others into the emotional maelstrom they create, and can vacillate between being victims and being the victimizers fluidly.

The world is full of genuine victims—people who have been hurt badly. But, there are also other types of people in the world who make victimization a state of mind. They reframe situations to reflect their own views. They think that everything is done to them. They refuse to take responsibility for their actions and blame others for them instead. They think that others take advantage of them and that people are out to get them for reasons unknown to anybody who asks them.

THIS MEANS THAT WHENEVER WE, as normal human beings who make mistakes, deny responsibility for our behavior and actions, we start acting like victims. We feel that others do not understand us and that they take advantage of us. This kind of thinking is dangerous. Any person who denies responsibility for their actions can become a part of people who have this kind of mentality.

Martyr Complex

> If it is never our fault, we cannot take responsibility for it. If we cannot take responsibility for it, we will always be its victim.
>
> —Richard Bach

A PERSON who has a martyr complex is similar to a person who has a victim complex; however, there are some differences between them. Contrary to self-claimed victims, people with a martyr complex either act like a martyr —someone who suffers persecution—for their own agenda or to avoid responsibility in order to feed either a psychological need or some other desire. They go out of their way to seek out suffering and pain. An individual may like the feeling of being a martyr and may create negative experiences in order to blame other people and cause sorrow, and guilt.

CONSIDER an example of a woman whose husband is a gambler who spends all his money at bars and frequents casinos in order to make more. He loves his wife and listens to her, but she never says anything to him about his habits, preferring to ignore them. However, she talks about her husband's behavior behind his back with her friends and complains to them that he gambles all the time, when in fact she is the one who is enabling her husband's gambling and continuing to complain about it.

She is the one who is not doing anything about it. She is sitting on her hands and waiting for the situation to resolve itself.

This woman is a prime example of someone who has a martyr complex. She ignores the negative consequences of her actions and creates, emphasizes, and exaggerates a negative experience so she can place blame on another person. She does not stop her husband from doing an action that is harmful even though she knows better. She is suffering persecution, in her eyes, by living with such a man, and complains about him to her friends to show how hard her life is.

People who behave this way do not accept any responsibility for their actions, and instead try to blame others for actions that they would have the power to stop if they just spoke up. They regularly put themselves in situations that are harmful for them, which produce negative passions such as resentment, hatred, anger, etc.

. . .

If we look at the bare bones of these concepts, we can see that they are based on the lack of acceptance of responsibility of one's actions. Both people suffering from victim syndrome and martyr syndrome try their hardest to avoid taking responsibility by shifting blame, guilt tripping, blaming others for their own actions, lying, cheating, and being moody. Therefore, only by taking, not avoiding, responsibility can an individual progress forward from their own mistakes. If they have committed an action that is heinous, then they should take responsibility for it and repent. They should analyze their actions with a critical eye and find out what prompted then to take such steps instead of wallowing in the despair that the world is out to get them or trying to blame others for their mistakes.

Therefore, any man who has committed any wrong should accept the responsibility for their actions in order to move forward. Self-pity and victimization can seem like an attractive pastime. Shifting blame can help prolong the belief that a person who has committed moral wrongs is, in fact, correct, when they actually are not. Lies can make life easier. But, forgiveness cannot be sought by any of these actions. Forgiveness should not be given to a wrongdoer if they do not realize the extent of their actions. If forgiveness is given before this realization, then it deteriorates the self-respect of the victim and makes the actions taken against them seem paltry. It renders the wrongs done to them morally right.

THUS, if an individual, who has committed wrongs, wishes to attain forgiveness, then they should accept responsibility for their actions, not because they wish to, but because they have to in order to achieve their goal.

> "This above all: to thine own self be true,
>
> And it must follow, as the night the day,
>
> Thou canst not then be false to any man."
>
> — William Shakespeare

3

GUILT AND REGRET: HOW THEY HELP.

> "Give sorrow words; the grief that does not speak knits up the o-er wrought heart and bids it break."
>
> — William Shakespeare

ALL INDIVIDUALS MAKE MISTAKES IN THEIR LIVES. Many times, these mistakes have significant consequences. Some things hurt others or impact others in ways that could not have been predicted. These things can be something as small as hurtful words to mistakes that lead to death. Guilt and remorse are two emotions that individuals feel in the aftermath of such mistakes. These emotions show the dissatisfaction of a person with their actions.

Guilt and Regret: The Road Back from Evil

> "No one who, like me, conjures up the most evil of those half-tamed demons that inhabit the human beast, and seeks to wrestle with them, can expect to come through the struggle unscathed."
>
> —Sigmund Freud

What are Guilt and Regret?

Guilt is an emotion that occurs when an individual realizes that the actions they have taken have compromised moral, ethical and legal standards and principles. The individual realizes that they have done wrong and that they bear the responsibility for it. They realize that they have done something that they should not have done. They feel anxiety, self-loathing, and shame towards their actions, which can prompt from them virtuous behavior, such as restraint, avoidance of self-indulgence, and harshness. If an individual feels guilty when they harm others or fail to be kind, the likelihood of them harming others decreases dramatically.

GUILT IS CLOSELY RELATED to shame. Guilt is felt when the personal morals of a person are violated, whereas shame is felt due to negative perceptions formed by people. Both directly influence each other. Shame can heighten guilt, while guilt can do the opposite. According to Mason and Fossum, "...guilt is a painful feeling of regret and responsibility for one's actions, shame is a painful feeling about oneself as a person". This means that shame comes from without, while guilt comes from within, and both act on each other every time.

. . .

If someone causes harm to others and feels guilty about their actions, they can be forgiven. Therefore, guilt facilitates forgiveness.

Consider the example of a woman who stole a diamond ring from her grandmother. The woman thought that she was desperate when she was doing the act. She thought that her grandmother would not mind. She knew that stealing was wrong but she felt that she would understand that her niece needed the ring more. However, that ring was an heirloom given to her grandmother by her father. When the girl learns that she does not need the ring anymore, she realizes the error of her actions. She realizes that what she did was wrong, morally and lawfully. She stole something from her grandmother, something which she might have gotten if she had just asked. When she sees her grandmother searching around desperately for that ring, she realizes the impact of her actions and feels incredible guilt at what she has done. She had vowed to never take anything from family, but in a moment of weakness, she had done so. She also feels guilty because she broke her word to herself.

. . .

In his example, the girl is feeling guilty because she broke moral laws and her personal code of conduct. She knew that the actions she was taking were wrong when she did them, but instead she rationalized it. However, as time passes she realizes that she hurt someone she loves and takes responsibility for her actions. This realization prompts her guilt.

This means that in order to establish guilt, one has to violate moral, ethical, or legal tenants and take responsibility for one's actions, along with realizing that a wrong has been committed. An individual also has to be aware of the wrongness of their actions before they take them. Only when these reasons are satisfied will guilt be established.

Regret, on the other hand, is the negative, self-focused emotion an individual experiences when they look back on their previous actions and realize they should have done something different because the result of their actions was not very good. The intensity of regret varies over time, and it depends on the self-control of an individual. A person under the grip of regret blames themselves for their actions, which prompts them to perform corrective actions and make their wrongs right. A person can be part of a situation that caused harm to others and may regret their involvement even if their actions were involuntary, innocent, or unintentional, or they can actively perform an action and regret it later because they believe they should have made better choices.

REGRET REVOLVES around past situations that an individual wishes they could have improved upon. These regrets can stem from unfortunate events or inevitable and unforeseen circumstances, none of which hold the individual responsible for their actions. Due to this, the individuals may wish that these things had not happened, no matter if they could have stopped them or not. They feel responsible for their actions and self-incriminate. Regrets can also stem from tragedies of luck rather than intention. For example, not being in the right place at the right time.

CONSIDER the example of a friend who broke an important promise. Several years ago,

Thomas promised his friend Dylan that he would always be there for him in a time of need. However, when Thomas actually needed Dylan, he could not come. Unfortunately, Dylan's wife had a heart attack the same day his friend Thomas crashed into a car and became paralyzed. When Dylan got the call from his friend, he remembered his promise but he told his friend that he could not come and help him because his vow was superseded by another vow.

YEARS LATER, Dylan felt incredible regret for breaking his promise to his friend. He believed rationally that he could not have done anything different, yet at the same time he felt like he should have done more, tried harder to find a solution. This is an example of regret due to tragedy of luck. Dylan was faced with two tragedies in one that he could not have predicted by any means, and these tragedies influences his ability to make decisions. They essentially tied his hands.

LET'S TAKE ANOTHER EXAMPLE. Suppose Alissa's grandmother is very ill, and she receives a call from her parents that she may not live long. They also tell her that her grandmother wishes to see her "little pea" very much. Unfortunately, Alyssa at that time is going through some hard times, so she thinks that she will postpone for a few days and then go. She lies to her parents about work and how busy she is because of it. They excuse her, but when she wakes up the next day, she finds that her grandmother has died during the night.

ALISSA FEELS regretful of her actions. She feels that she could have and should have done more rather than wallowing in her misery. She should not have lied to her granny. Alyssa's regret stems from the fact that her actions resulted in a disastrous ending. She wishes she could have improved on that situation, but she could not. Alyssa's example of regret stems from her intentional action of not going to visit her grandmother. Due to this decision, she feels immense regret.

BOTH OF THESE examples show that regret can stem from many reasons, but usually it stems from a wish to improve upon past actions in a situation that turned out to be not very favorable for an individual at all.

Forgiveness: How Grief and Regret Help

Regret can prompt a person to do better in their future actions. They may be more careful when making a choice. They may try to glean every possibility, and they may think twice before making a decision. A wrongdoer who shows regret at their past actions can improve upon themselves, accept the responsibility for their actions, and make better decisions. They may realize which choices could lead to morally grey actions that could jeopardize their sense of self.

Conversely, guilt can do the same thing. As mentioned before, guilt is the emotion people feel when they realize that they have done something wrong that breaks moral and ethical bounds. Something they should not have done. A guilty conscience may prompt a person to do better, to take actions that do not harm others in the future. Guilt also enables a wrongdoer to seek forgiveness because only when a wrong-doer realizes their mistake can they be forgiven by their victim without compromising their self-respect.

THEREFORE, in the end, grief and regret can help a person become a better version of themselves. They can also help wrongdoers realize the depths of their actions and show them that they themselves carry the responsibility for every action they have taken, and only in accepting their actions can they become better and gain forgiveness from those they transgressed against.

4

ANGER MANAGEMENT: ON A MICRO SCALE.

"Anybody can become angry — that is easy, but to be angry with the right person and to the right degree and at the right time and for the right purpose, and in the right way — that is not within everybody's power and is not easy."

— Aristotle

ANGER IS AN EMOTION THAT IS RELATED TO hurt and fear. When considered positive, it is viewed as a protective response towards a perceived threat. When considered negative, it is known as aggression. It is a psychological defense that, while protecting our ego, makes far more problems than it solves. Anger in a way is not a primary emotion; there are many hurt emotions lying underneath it, such as guilt, rejection, powerlessness, devaluation, unimportance, disregard, and accusation, among others.

Anger causes a reduction in an individuals' cognitive and information-processing ability. This reduction in cognitive capacity can prompt angry individuals to make risky decisions. Anger makes people less trusting and makes them think negatively about others. Angry people are also more likely to show correspondence bias. They are also more likely to blame another person for their misery. An individual in the throes of anger can destroy relationships, harmony, and trust, because they try to alleviate their feelings of hurt, fear, guilt on another person rather than talking to them like an adult.

. . .

Anger can also harm a person's self-esteem; It can make them say or do things that they will regret later. Uncontrolled anger has also been shown to damage a person's health and life expectancy because it elevates blood pressure and increases the heart rate, and triggers the body's fight or flight response. An angry person may lose their empathy, thoughtfulness, and objectivity and may cause harm to themselves or others. Anger can also influence aggression and can increase its intensity or probability.

Since it has been mentioned above that anger reduces cognitive capacity, then it is easy to infer that angry people make decisions that are more likely to harm than help them. They make choices while they are angry that might lead them to do things that they had not wanted to do in the first place. They may commit an immoral action with a malicious intention that could be labeled as evil because it might cause serious, excessive harm to another fellow human beings.

. . .

Therefore, it is crucial to understand the cause or causes of our anger and the effects of venting out the emotion itself because anger is more destructive than it is helpful. It can harm people irrevocably because under the influence of anger individuals utter words which can render their victims helpless, disregarded, and demeaned.

Anger Management: Goals

People deal with anger in different ways, some shout, some close up, and others get cold. The individuals who are more likely to shout usually have a low tolerance for frustration which leads them to feel annoyed easily. They can get angry easily and can lash out at others without thinking about their actions. The people may try to curtail their anger by smothering it and by venting it out on themselves or in their work. This may even work for a while, however, if these individuals cannot control themselves when they are angry, they may need anger management counseling.

. . .

Anger management aims to help people with the management of their anger. They are a set of strategies used to reduce the emotional impact and causes of anger. These strategies aim to reduce the harmful effects of anger. They try to curtail the volatility of a person and help them handle their emotions so they can take rational, not emotional, decisions. They can help individuals recognize the underlying problems in their minds and can help them target the reasons behind their anger. For example, teenagers usually get angry because they are misunderstood or not being heard, while adults can get angry for many reasons from abuse to loss of control.

Some advice followed by angry individuals while going through anger management regimens can be thinking before speaking, only expressing anger when calm, not holding grudges, relaxing when feeling angry, taking a short break, and trying to use humor to lighten the situation, among others. These regimens can help people diffuse arguments, resolve disagreements, target positive resolutions rather than focusing on the anger, identify situations that trigger anger, circumvent getting angry, and teach them to live with their anger.

When people get frustrated with some issues, they get angry. This anger can result in physical fights, shouting matches, and even harmful acts from abuse and persecution to murder and rape. The potential harms of anger are many if anger is left unsubdued. Anger management allays these fears and can help a person manage themselves and their anger by providing coping strategies that they can use to make sure they are never out of control.

Conclusion

Anger management can help people take control of their anger and can help them channel it into better avenues. These strategies teach angry individuals to manage, diffuse, target the cause of their anger, resolve the triggers of the anger peacefully, and may even teach them how to not get angry through various techniques such as counting down to 0 from 100, going on a walk to burn off anger, ruminating on the causes of anger, walking away when very angry, and using humor to manage anger.

If a person has committed a wrongdoing and asked for forgiveness, but gets angry every time their transgressions are raised, they should try to control their anger. Anger reduces cognitive capacity, which makes it very likely for a person to say or do things that may hurt or harm others. The wrongdoer should concentrate on making sure that they do not offend people further when they are under the influence of anger.

5

CULTIVATION OF PEACE AND CALM.

"Letting go gives us freedom, and freedom is the only condition for happiness. If, in our heart, we still cling to anything - anger, anxiety, or possessions - we cannot be free."

— Thich Nhat Hanh

AS HUMAN BEINGS WE ARE AFFECTED BY OUR expectations. We move through the world with a wealth of expectations following us, impacting our perception, and influencing our choices. These expectations or hopes frame the way we interpret events or situations in our lives. When these expectations are shattered or broken, vindicative passions, such as anger, wrath, fury, etc., rise up. These passions can lure us towards the dark side and can prompt us to commit actions that can be classified as evil actions—actions from which there is no coming back.

THEREFORE, in order to maintain our peace and to remain vigilant of the slide down into darkness, every individual should cultivate peace and calm in their soul. Peace and calm can help us remain calm when things don't go how we expected them to go. They can also help develop the capacity to expect everything so that we will never be disappointed. Thus, peace and calm can help humanity skirt the worst of the temptation towards the dark side.

> "We live in the middle of things which have all been destined to die. Mortal have you been born, to mortals have you given birth. Reckon on everything, expect everything."
>
> —Seneca

PEACE IS a deliberate state of calm that results from the exclusion of vindicative passions and stressful emotions, such as anger, anxiety, resentment, shame, and disappointment, among others. Being at peace can bring serenity and calmness to a person's thoughts. They may be able to think clearly, take just decisions, see further possibilities, consider more angles of an issue, and stay unperturbed during times of distress.

. . .

THE FEELING of peace is produced by calmness. Calm is a state of mind from which every disturbance is excluded—a mind that is serene. This state of calmness is achieved through relaxation, such as during meditation, prayer, or while lying down. Calmness can be increased through practice. It can be trained to become better over time until a peaceful mind is not distracted by emotions or any stimuli around it. Negative emotions are the bane of this state of mind; they can destroy the rhythm built by relaxation.

A PEACEFUL MIND can cause the brain to release "good" hormones, which relax an individual's emotional and physical state and can promote good health. Conversely, a calm mind can reduce the production of "bad" hormones such as cortisol which harm the body. A peaceful mind can make a person more in control of their emotions, which makes angry bursts, hasty decisions, and unclear expectation highly unlikely. It can grant a person clarity, so their goals and vision are clearer than ever. By developing inner peace, serenity and trust, a person can gain better control over themselves and their emotions; they can also gain wisdom and can become self-reflective. Such a mind also protects a person from committing evil actions because it makes things clearer for them and improves their self-control.

Conclusion

IN THE END, a calm and peaceful state of mind can help an individual acquire more control over their emotions and themselves. It makes them less prone to be distracted by stimuli around and inside them. They can achieve a greater clarity through a peaceful state of mind, which improves decision-making, reducing the likelihood of making disastrous decisions. A calm mind also affords a person many health benefits as it increases the production of good hormones in the body, which can make a person seem younger and healthier.

ABOUT THE AUTHOR

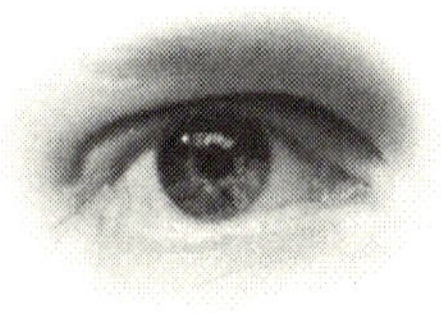

SNIPPETS OF LITERATURE *CLUB* is a team of professional and amateur writers, spread all over the world but connected by the passion of making **valuable products.**

If you enjoyed this book, please take a few moments to write a review of it. Thank you!

As you know, maintaining a top rating is vital for writers like us to keep supporting our families, especially in these difficult times. We personally depend on this and we always aim to offer the best products we can. That said, we are only human beings.

Kind Regards

SNIPPETS OF LITERATURE *CLUB*

REFERENCES

Aquinas, Thomas. On Evil: St. Thomas Aquinas. Edited and translated by John A.

Arendt, Hannah. Eichmann in Jerusalem: A Report on the Banality of Evil. Rev. ed. New York: Penguin, 1965.

Bernstein, Richard J. Radical Evil: A Philosophical Interrogation. Cambridge: Polity

Press, 2002.

. . .

Cohn, Norman. Europe's Inner Demons. London: Paladin, 1976.

Forbrath, Peter. The River Congo: The Discovery, Exploration, and Exploitation of the World's Most Dramatic Rivers. Harper & Row, Publishers, 1977

Graham, Gordon. Evil and Christian Ethics. Cambridge: Cambridge University Press, 2001.

Kekes, John. The Roots of Evil. 2005 edition. Cornell University Press

Kekes, John. Why Robespierre Chose Terror: The lesson of the first totalitarian revolution. Published in CJ Magazine in Spring 2006

Kant, Immanuel. Religion within the Limits of Reason Alone. 1794. Translated by T. M.

. . .

Hobbes, Thomas. Leviathan. 1651. London: Dent, 1962.

Leibniz, Gottfried Wilhelm. Theodicy. 1875–90. Translated by E. M. Huggard.

Loomis, Stanley. Paris in the Terror. Philadelphia: Lippincott, 1964.

Mill, John Stuart. The Subjection of Women. 1869.

Morton, Adam. On Evil. New York: Routledge, 2004.

Nietzsche, Friedrich. Beyond Good and Evil. 1886.

Plato. The Republic. Translated by Desmond Lee with an introduction by Melissa Lane. Penguin Classics; 2nd Edition, 2007.

. . .

Russell, Bertrand. The Conquest of Happiness. 1930. London: Routledge, 1993.

Rousseau, Jean-Jacques. Emile. 1780. Translated by Barbara Foxley. London: Dent,

1974.

Schama, Simon. Citizens. New York: Knopf, 1989.

Freud, Sigmund. Beyond the Pleasure Principle. 1920. Translated by James Strachey.

New York: Bantam, 1959.

Manufactured by Amazon.ca
Bolton, ON

20924528R10169